Phve

Documents and Debates
The German Reformation

Documents and Debates
General Editor: John Wroughton M.A., F.R.Hist.S

The German Reformatio

Katherine Leach

Head of History,
The Royal School, Bath

MACMILLAN

First published 1991

1903509194

Published by
MACMILLAN EDUCATION LTD
Houndmills, Basingstoke, Hampshire RG21 2XS
and London
Companies and representatives
throughout the world

Printed in Hong Kong

British Library Cataloguing in Publication Data
Leach, Katherine
The German Reformation
1. Germany. Christian Church. Reformation
I. Title   II. Series
274.3
ISBN 0–333–48562–9

The cover illustration of Martin Luther is from the Museo Poldi-Pezzoli
and is reproduced by kind permission of the Mansell Collection.

90 04

Contents

General Editor's Preface

This book forms part of a series entitled *Documents and Debates*, which is aimed primarily at sixth formers. The earlier volumes in the series each covered approximately one century of history, using material both from original documents and from modern historians. The more recent volumes, however, are designed in response to the changing trends in history examinations at 18 plus, most of which now demand the study of documentary sources and the testing of historical skills. Each volume therefore concentrates on a particular topic within a narrow span of time. It consists of eight sections, each dealing with a major theme in depth, illustrated by extracts drawn from primary sources. The series intends partly to provide experience for those pupils who are required to answer questions on documentary material at A-level, and partly to provide pupils of all abilities with a digestible and interesting collection of source material, which will extend the normal textbook approach.

This book is designed essentially for the pupil's own personal use. The author's introduction will put the period as a whole into perspective, highlighting the central issues, main controversies, available source material and recent developments. Although it is clearly not our intention to replace the traditional textbook, each section will carry its own brief introduction, which will set the documents into context. A wide variety of source material has been used in order to give the pupils the maximum amount of experience – letters, speeches, newspapers, memoirs, diaries, official papers, Acts of Parliament, Minute Books, accounts, local documents, family papers, etc. The questions vary in difficulty, but aim throughout to compel the pupil to think in depth by the use of unfamiliar material. Historical Knowledge and understanding will be tested, as well as basic comprehension. Pupils will also be encouraged by the questions to assess the reliability of evidence, to recognise bias and emotional prejudice, to reconcile conflicting accounts and to extract the essential from the irrelevant. Some questions, *marked with an asterisk*, require knowledge outside the immediate extract and are intended for further research or discussion, based on the pupil's general knowledge of the period. Finally, we hope that students using this material will learn something of the nature of historical inquiry and the role of the historian.

John Wroughton

Acknowledgements

The author and publishers wish to thank the following who have kindly given permission for the use of copyright material:

Edward Arnold for extracts from *Luther: Documents in Modern History*, ed. E. G. Rupp and B. Drewery, 1970; and the *German Nation and Martin Luther* by A. G. Dickens, 1974.

Augsburg Fortress Publishers for extracts from *Works of Martin Luther*, Vols 3 and 4 © 1931 Muhlenberg Press.

Epworth Press for extracts from *Patterns of Reformation* by Gorden Rupp, 1969.

Penguin Books Ltd for extracts from *The Imitation of Christ* by Thomas à Kempis, translated by Leo Sherley-Price, 1952.

SCM Press for extracts from *Melanchthon and Bucer*, edited by W. Pauck, Library of Christian Classics XIX, 1969.

Yale University Press for extracts from *Reformation in the Cities* by Steven B. Ozment, 1975.

Every effort has been made to trace all the copyright-holders, but if any have been inadvertently overlooked the publishers will be pleased to make the necessary arrangements at the first opportunity.

The German Reformation

'Apart from Luther the Reformation itself cannot be understood. . . . Indeed, whether but for Luther the Reform movement of the sixteenth century would have swept over Europe in the way it did is highly questionable. What he achieved was rendered possible because the time and the milieu were matched in him by the man also.' (B. M. G. Reardon). What was there in the time and the milieu, as well as the man, which cased such an upheaval?

There was no doubt in many people's minds about the corruption of the Catholic, or universal, church. This was particularly felt in Germany, where the clergy had many privileges and owned much property and yet were generally perceived not to be doing their duty adequately. One consequence was the increasing number of preachers paid by local communities, who helped to prepare the ground for Luther. Papal taxation was another grievance, so that Luther's attack on the position of the pope appealed to those who resented clerical corruption and those whose nationalism appreciated the assault on Rome. At the same time there was a genuine popular anxiety about the possibility of salvation, an anxiety which showed itself in the establishment of new religious endowments, and in payments for private masses and indulgences.

It can also be argued that the Reformation was a much wider movement than this, that it occurred, for example, because the economic problems of the early sixteenth century, especially the rising population, meant that the peasants were overstretched and so welcomed an end of payments to Rome while the princes could gain from taking over church land. Equally it can be argued that the princes were more concerned with the political gains of breaking with Rome, but neither economics nor politics can provide a complete explanation. The influence of the Renaissance is another factor in the situation and there can be no doubt about the importance of the humanists. They challenged the Catholic church, which tended to downgrade the importance of Scripture and exalted church traditions instead, including teachings about purgatory, indulgences and clerical celibacy, an emphasis which Luther was notably to reverse. Their Biblical studies, and especially Erasmus's 1516 edition of the New Testament, had an immense influence on Luther and others; the study of Scripture was to be central to Luther's life and teaching and a basic tenet of all Protestantism.

It is difficult to appreciate the importance of the Reformation to ordinary people without some understanding of how pervasive the church was in everyday life. Everyone was assumed to be a member of the church as well as the state, it was not a matter for individual decision before Luther; church festivals were the only holidays, and in many other ways life was organised by the church. Thus it was much easier for Luther, a dominant and determined character, to make an impact than it would be today. He was a most effective preacher and teacher, who made a permanent mark on Germany through his writings, his translation of the Bible and his hymns, and it is certainly true to say that without him the German Reformation would not have been as successful as it was and, indeed, might never have happened.

What was Luther's message, that had such an effect? From the beginning Luther was convinced that his mission was to return the Christian church to what it had been in Biblical times and undo the 'innovations', as he saw them, that had been introduced during the intervening centuries. Justification by faith alone, his central doctrine, was inimical to the church's emphasis on man's contribution to his own salvation. He believed that God was offering salvation through Christ and so all man had to do was accept. This was bad enough for the church authorities, but the idea of the priesthood of all believers was revolutionary in that it downgraded the clergy until they were no more than ordinary men doing an ordinary, though important, job. The various corollaries of this, such as the acceptability of clerical marriage, combined with the emphasis on Scripture already mentioned, were the cause of much of the opposition to Luther. His teachings on the sacraments, reducing them to only two (even though the Anabaptists were able to argue that his acceptance of infant baptism was unscriptural), his denial of transubstantiation and his introduction of services in the vernacular further widened the split between his position and that of Rome. The increasingly common use of printing helped substantially to spread knowledge of those ideas as printers seized eagerly on anything that could be associated with Luther, and so compromise between the two sides became less and less possible.

The cities of Germany were the first to take up Luther's ideas, in an uncoordinated way, and often adapted them to suit themselves; Martin Bucer in Strasbourg, for example, took ideas from both Luther and Zwingli for his reformed church. In the countryside, too, Luther was quickly taken up but his attack on the peasants, at the time of the revolt, lost him much of their support. In the long term, the princes were the most important for the spread of Lutheranism, especially as it has been established that only about ten per cent of the German people became really convinced believers. The princes took advantage of the Emperor Charles V's preoccupations elsewhere to gain control of the church in their own states and even the emperor's victory over them at Muhlberg in 1547 made little difference. The Confession of Augsburg, largely the work of Luther's colleague Philip Melanchthon in 1530, was an attempt to stress what Catholics and Lutherans had in common and so reunite them, but it became instead the official creed of the Lutheran church and this position was confirmed twenty-five years later in the Treaty of Augsburg, which for the first time authorised the existence of two religions in the Empire, even if individual freedom was limited for most people to acceptance of one's ruler's religion.

The survival of Lutheranism can therefore be seen as a political development, but it is one which owes its origins to 'a single monk', as Charles V called him, who dared to put forward his own ideas in contradiction to contemporary authority and thereby changed the history of Europe.

Bibliography

R.H. Bainton, *The Reformation of the Sixteenth Century*
A.G. Dickens, *Reformation and Society in Sixteenth Century Europe*
A.G. Dickens, *The German Nation and Martin Luther*
A.E. McGarth, *Reformation Thought: An Introduction*
K. Randell, *Luther and the German Reformation, 1517–55*
B.M.G. Reardon, *Religious Thought in the Reformation*
E.G. Rupp, *Patterns of Reformation*
R.W. Scribner, *The German Reformation*
G.H. Williams, *The Radical Reformation*
J. Atkinson, *Martin Luther and the Birth of Protestantism*
R.H. Bainton, *Here I Stand: A Life of Martin Luther*
A.G. Dickens, *Martin Luther and the Reformation*
V.H.H. Green, *Luther and the Reformation*
J.K. Kittelson, *Luther the Reformer*
M. Mullett, *Luther*

I The Background to the Reformation

It is probably impossible to define precisely the 'causes' of the Reformation, although many attempts have been made from various points of view. This chapter is, therefore, concerned with the 'background' – that is, some of the factors which helped to create a climate of opinion in which church reform became possible, though it is important to realise that reform was never inevitable. The church had survived previous periods of difficulty with its universality intact, so that no one could have expected Luther's attack on the sale of indulgences to lead to a permanent rift in Christendom.

There was criticism of the church in the early sixteenth century, including criticism of the corruption of popes, bishops, etc., by those who had the opportunity to experience it. There was much anticlericalism among ordinary people, who disliked in particular the financial exactions of the clergy, and this, in Germany, was mingled with growing national feeling in opposition to taxation by the foreign papacy. At the same time there was little criticism of the doctrines or teachings of the church. The '*devotio moderna*', which developed in the Netherlands and Rhineland during the fifteenth century, offered a different way of life for Christians with its emphasis on holy living. It was not a reforming movement but rather a turning-away from the ordinary church with the intention of reviving faith among its membership, but it did provide an alternative model to the church as it was generally perceived.

Humanism was another important factor for the Reformation. Biblical scholars provided better texts for students to study and presented new ideas. Erasmus was, of course, the most famous of the humanists and was also a very important and effective critic of the church, so much so that he was, in later life, accused of being a Lutheran, a charge he indignantly denied, although he did admire some aspects of Luther's work, see Chapter VI, extract 1.

All these factors combined to make it possible for Luther to have a major impact on the church in Germany and beyond and so helped to 'cause' the Reformation, but it is important to remember that much more was involved and that, in particular, social and economic developments have been ignored here, as has the invention and spread of the printing press, without which Luther's ideas could not have been so quickly and widely disseminated.

1 An Early Attack on the Church

The hour will come for all faithful Christians to witness the establishment of the rightful order. Let everyone join the ranks of the pious who will pledge themselves to observe it. It is plain that the Holy Father, the Pope, and all our princes have abandoned the task set them by God. It may be that God has appointed a man to set things right. Let no one, neither princes nor cities, make excuses for not heeding God's warnings. . . .

Take a good look at how bishops act nowadays. They make war and cause unrest in the world; they behave like secular lords, which is, of course, what they are. And the money for this comes from pious donations that ought to go to honest parish work, and not to be spent on war. I agree with a remark made by Duke Frederick of Austria to the Emperor Sigismund in Basel: 'Bishops are blind; it is up to us to open their eyes'. . . .

It seems to me that great evils have arisen in the western part of Christendom since Pope Calixtus imposed the rule of celibacy. It may be a good thing for a man to keep himself pure, but observe the wickedness now going on in the Church! Many priests have lost their livings because of women. Or they are secret sodomites. All the hatred existing between priests and laymen is due to this. In sum: secular priests ought to be allowed to marry. In marriage they will live more piously and honourably, and the friction between them and the laity will disappear.

Reformatio Sigismundi, c.1438, in J. Lotherington (ed.), *Years of Renewal*, 1988, p. 137

Questions

a How might the 'Reformatio Sigismundi' have affected attitudes towards Luther and his enemies (lines 1–5)?

b What does the second paragraph (lines 8–14) have in common with Luther's 'Address to the Christian Nobility of the German Nation'?

c Why should hatred between priests and laymen be due to celibacy (lines 19–23)? How might this attack on clerical celibacy have helped to prepare the way for Luther?

2 The Renaissance Papacy

(a) He [the future Pope Alexander VI] is a fluent speaker, writes well – though not in a literary style; is extremely astute and very energetic and skilful in business matters. He is enormously wealthy, and through his connections with kings and princes, commands great influence. He has built a beautiful and comfortable palace for himself between the Bridge of Sant' Angelo and the Campo di Fiori. His revenues from his papal offices, his abbeys in Italy and Spain, his three bishoprics of Valencia, Portus and Cartagena, are vast. His office of Vice-Chancellor alone

yields him 8000 ducats annually. His plate, his pearls, his stuffs
10 embroidered with silk and gold, his books are all of such quality as
would befit a king or pope. I need hardly mention the sumptuous bed-
hangings, trappings for his horses and similar things of gold, silver, and
silk, nor the vast quantity of gold coin which he possesses. Altogether, it
is believed that he possesses more gold and riches of every sort than all
15 the cardinals put together.

Jacopo da Volterra, *Diairio Romano 1479–1484*, ed. by E. Carusi

(b) So died Pope Alexander [VI], at the height of glory and prosperity
about whom it must be known that he was a man of the utmost power
and of great judgment and spirit, as his actions and behavior showed.
But as his first accession to the Papacy was foul and shameful – for he
20 bought with gold so high an office – so similarly his government was in
agreement with its vile foundation. There was in him, and in full
measure, all vices both of flesh and spirit. There was in him no
religion, no keeping of his word. He promised all things liberally, but
bound himself to nothing that was not useful to himself. He had no care
25 for justice, since in his days Rome was a den of thieves and murderers.
His ambition was boundless, and such that it grew in the same measure
as his state increased. Nevertheless, his sins meeting with no punishment
in this world, he was to the last of his days most prosperous. In one
word, he was more evil and more lucky than, perhaps, any other pope
30 for many ages before.

Francesco Guicciardini, *Storia d'Italia*, Chapter 27

(c) It seems to have been [Leo X's] intention to pass his time cheerfully
and to secure himself against trouble and anxiety by all the means in his
power. He therefore sought all opportunities of pleasure and hilarity and
indulged his leisure in amusements, jests and singing – either from a
35 natural liking for this kind of pastime or because he believed that by
avoiding vexation and care he might thereby lengthen his days.

Paolo Giovio, *La Vita di Dicenove Huomini Illustri*, trans. by
L. Domenichi.

(d) No man is more disgusted than I am with the ambition, the avarice,
and the profligacy of the priests. . . . Nevertheless, my position at the
court of several Popes forced me to desire their greatness for the sake of
40 my own interest. But, had it not been for this, I should have loved
Martin Luther as myself – not in order to free myself from the laws
which Christianity lays upon us but in order to see this swarm of
scoundrels put back into their proper place, so that they may be forced
to live without vice or without power.

Francesco Guicciardini, *Counsels and Reflections*, trans. by N.H.
Thomson.

[All these extracts from E. R. Chamberlin, *The Bad Popes*, 1970, pp. 166–
7, 204, 218, 245]

6   THE GERMAN REFORMATION

45 **(e)** Rome is a harlot. I would not take a thousand gulden not to have seen it, for I never would have believed the true state of affairs from what other people told me, had I not seen it myself. The Italians mocked us for being pious monks, for they hold Christians fools. They say six or seven masses in the time it takes me to say one, for they take money for

50 it and I do not. The only crime in Italy is poverty. They still punish homicide and theft a little, for they have to, but no other sin is too gross for them. . . .

So great and bold is Roman impiety that neither God nor man, neither sin nor shame, is feared. All good men who have seen Rome

55 bear witness to this; all bad ones come back worse than before.

Martin Luther in P. Smith, *The Life and Letters of Martin Luther*, 1911, p. 19

Questions

 a   In what ways do these extracts suggest that Alexander VI and Leo X were not fit to be popes?

★ *b*   Was there anything creditable about the reigns of these popes?

 c   Why does Guicciardini, in extract **(d)**, say that he agrees with Luther but cannot become a Lutheran?

 d   What does Luther mean by saying that 'the only crime in Italy is poverty' (line 50)?

★ *e*   How important do you think were the characters and style of the popes of this period in causing Luther's revulsion against the Roman Catholic Church and, in general, in creating a climate in which Luther could receive support for his attacks on Rome?

3   A Letter from Rome

Magister Berthold Hackerling: to Magister Ortwin Gratius.
Brotherly love, by way of salutation.
Honoured Sir, having in remembrance the promise I made you on parting, that I would tell you all the news, and how I fared, I would

5 have you know that I have now been two months at Rome, but as yet have found no patron. An assessor of the Rota would fain have bespoken me, and I was well pleased, and said, 'I am nothing loth, Sir: but I pray your magnificence to apprize me what my charge will be.' He replied, that my lodgment would be in the stable, to minister unto a

10 mule, serve it with victuals and drink, curry-comb it, and keep it clean; and that I must have a care that he was ready to carry his master, with bridle and saddle and so forth. And then it would be my office to run by his side to the court, and home again.

Thereupon I made answer that it was not meet for me, who am a

15 Master of Arts of Cologne, to drudge thus. Quoth he, 'If not, the loss is yours.' I am resolved, therefore, to return to the fatherland. I, to curry-comb a mule and mundify a stable! The Devil run away with the stable

and the mule! I verily believe it would be flying in the face of the
Statutes of the University! For a Magister must needs comport himself
20   as a Magister. It would be a scandalous thing for a Master of Arts of
Cologne to do such drudgery. Nay, for the honour of the University I
will return to the fatherland.

Rome moreover pleaseth me not in other ways. You would not
believe how arrogant are the Clerks and Curialists. One of them said but
25   yesterday that he would besquatter a Cologne Magister. 'Besquatter the
gallows!' quoth I. Then he made answer that he, too, was a Magister, to
wit of the Curia, and that a Magister of the Curia took precedence of a
Master of Arts of Germany. 'That', said I, 'is impossible. Would you
fain make yourself out my equal, seeing that you have never offered
30   yourself for examination, as did I when five Magisters sifted me with
rigour? You are naught but a Magister by diploma.'

Then began he to dispute with me, saying, 'And what is a Magister?'
'A Magister,' I answered, 'is a person duly qualified, promoted and
graduated in the Seven Liberal Arts, having first undergone a magistral
35   examination. . . .'

So, be well assured, I shall hie me back to Germany; for there
Magisters are paramount; and rightly. I can prove it by the Gospel:
Christ called himself Magister, and not Doctor, saying, 'Ye call me
Master and Lord, and ye say well, for so I am.'
40   But I can write no more, for paper faileth me . . . .
Farewell.

> Ulrich von Hutten, *Letters of Obscure Men*, 1516, in L.W. Spitz
> (ed.), *The Northern Renaissance*, 1972, pp. 36–7

Questions

a   Explain what is meant by a 'patron' (line 6), 'the Curia' (line 27),
    and 'the Seven Liberal Arts' (line 34).

b   The work from which this extract comes was a deliberate mockery
    of some scholars of the period. How is the supposed writer of this
    letter being mocked and does the mockery seem to you to be
    justified?

c   What evidence does this passage provide to show that Hutten was a
    leading proponent of German nationalism in the early sixteenth
    century?

d   How does the implicit criticism of Rome here compare with
    Luther's attack on Rome in extract 2(e) above?

4   Germany and Rome

We see that there is no gold and almost no silver in our German land.
What little may perhaps be left is drawn away daily by new schemes
invented by the council of the most holy members of the Roman Curia.
What is thus squeezed out of us is put to the most shameful uses. . . . Leo

X gives a part of it to his nephews and relations. A portion is consumed
by a host of most reverend cardinals (of which the Holy Father created
no fewer than one and thirty in a single day), as well as in supporting
innumerable referendaries, auditors, protonotaries, abbreviators, apostolic secretaries, chamberlains and a variety of officials forming the elite
of the great Head Church.

These in turn draw after them, at untold expense, copyists, beadles,
messengers, servants, scullions, mule-drivers, grooms and a countless
army of prostitutes and the most degraded followers. They maintain
dogs, horses, monkeys, long-tailed apes and many more such creatures
for their pleasure. They build houses all of marble . . . In short, a vast
number of the worst of men are supported in Rome in idle indulgence
by means of our money.

Does not your Grace now clearly perceive how many bold robbers,
how many cunning hypocrites, are engaged constantly in committing
the greatest crimes under cover of the monk's cowl, and how many
crafty hawks feign the simplicity of doves, and how many ravening
wolves simulate the innocence of lambs? And although there be a few
truly pious men among them, even they cling to superstitions and
pervert the law of life which Christ laid down for us.

Now if all these who devastate Germany and continue to devour
everything might once be driven out, and an end made of the unbridled
plundering, swindling and deception with which the Romans have
overwhelmed us, we should again have gold and silver in sufficiency
and should be able to keep it. And then this money might be put to
better uses, as to put on foot great armaments and extend the boundaries
of the empire; also to conquer the Turks, if this seems desirable; to
enable many who because of poverty now steal and rob to earn an
honest living once again; to give the starving contributions from the
state to mitigate their need; to help scholars, and to advance the study of
the arts and sciences and good literature; above all, to make it possible
that every virtue receive its reward, want to be relieved at home,
indolence banished and deceit destroyed.

Ulrich von Hutten to the Elector of Saxony, 1520, in
J.H. Robinson, *Readings in European History* Vol. II, 1906,
pp. 72–3

Questions

a What is meant by the 'Roman Curia' (line 3) and the 'great Head
   Church' (line 10)?

b Why does Hutten say that the money paid to the pope is put to 'the
   most shameful uses' (line 4)?

★ c Why should Hutten address this letter to the Elector of Saxony
      rather than to any of the other German princes?

★ *d* Which of Hutten's 'better uses' (line 30) for the money seem to you
to have been practicable at the time? Why did he think it might be
advisable to 'conquer the Turks' (line 31)?

e Do you think this extract would be effective as propaganda only or
could it be seen as an attempt to arouse the Elector and others to
take action?

5 An Expression of German Nationalism

I would not have considered it something special, most excellent fathers
and distinguished youth, that I, a German and your fellow countryman,
can speak to you in Latin, if those talents of our Germany still
flourished, and if that age had returned in which our ambassadors are
5   said to have spoken Greek rather than Latin. But, since through the
adverseness of the ages and the change of the times, not only amongst us
but even in Italy, the mother and ancient parent of letters, all the past
splendor of literature has perished or been extinguished, and all the
noble disciplines have been driven away and ruined by barbaric tumults,
10   I am not at all confident that, given the slowness of my mind and the
poverty of my powers, I can speak to you adequately in Latin. . . . I shall
hope for your indulgence if you consider a little man born in the midst
of barbarity and drunkenness, as they say, cannot speak so sensibly as is
required by your most sagacious ears.
15   O men of Germany, assume those ancient passions by which you
were so often a dread and terror to the Romans, and turn your eyes to
the wants of Germany and consider her lacerated and divided borders.
What a shame to have a yoke of servitude imposed on our nation and to
pay tributes and taxes to foreign and barbaric kings. O free and strong
20   people, O noble and brave nation, clearly worthy of the Roman
Empire, your renowned seaport [Danzig] is held by the Poles and your
ocean gateway is occupied by the Dane! In the east the most vigorous
tribes are held as slaves. . . . In the west, however, upper Gaul [France] is
so friendly and munificent toward us, thanks to the immortal virtue and
25   incredible wisdom of Philipp of the Rhenish Palatinate, who rules the
shore on either side of its renowned river and ever will rule with an
auspicious reign. . . . But in the south we are burdened with a kind of
distinguished servitude, for new colonies are continually being
established, thanks to the ancient and detestable avarice for fostering
30   luxuries by which our land is being emptied of its wonderful natural
resources, while we pay from the public treasury to others what we need
for ourselves. So determined is fortune or fate to pursue and destroy the
Germans, the remnants of the Roman Empire. But I fear I have
progressed more freely than I desire, so disgusted am I with my
35   Germany when I consider the things in the store of books, taken from
the Greeks and Latins and preserved by the power of our Emperors,
books which we have till now abandoned like the detested spoils of the

enemies, as if locked in a prison, covered with dust, untouched, and not well protected from the rain.

> Conrad Celtis, Inaugural Address to the University of Ingoldstadt, 1492, in L.W. Spitz (ed.), *The Northern Renaissance*, 1972, pp. 15, 19–20

Questions

a   What excuse does the author give for the possible inadequacy of his Latin? Does the language of this extract (even in translation) suggest that he needed to apologise for his use of the language?

b   What, according to the author, has happened to the reputation of Germany and why has this occurred?

c   Explain what 'kind of distinguished servitude' (lines 27–8) has been imposed on Germany and what has been the result for the country?

★ d   What contribution did nationalism make to the beginning and ultimate success of the German Reformation?

6   The Imitation of Christ

(a) On Personal Humility

Everyone naturally desires knowledge, but of what use is knowledge itself without fear of God? A humble countryman who serves God is more pleasing to Him than a conceited intellectual who knows the course of the stars, but neglects his own soul. A man who truly knows

5   himself realizes his own worthlessness, and takes no pleasure in the praises of men. Did I possess all knowledge in the world, but had no love, how would this help me before God, who will judge me by my deeds?

Restrain an inordinate desire for knowledge, in which is found much

10   anxiety and deception. Learned men always wish to appear so, and desire recognition of their wisdom. But there are many matters, knowledge of which brings little or no advantage to the soul. Indeed, a man is unwise if he occupies himself with any things save those that further his salvation.

15   The more complete and excellent your knowledge, the more severe will be God's judgement on you, unless your life be the more holy. Therefore, do not be conceited of any skill or knowledge that you possess, but respect the knowledge that is entrusted to you. If it seems to you that you know a great deal and have wide experience in many

20   fields, yet remember that there are many matters of which you are ignorant. So do not be conceited, but confess your ignorance. Why do you wish to esteem yourself above others, when there are many who are wiser and more perfect in the Law of God?

A true understanding and humble estimate of oneself is the highest

25   and most valuable of all lessons. To take no account of oneself, but always to think well and highly of others is the highest wisdom and

perfection. Should you see another person openly doing evil, or carrying out a wicked purpose, do not on that account consider yourself better than him, for you cannot tell how long you will remain in a state
30 of grace. We are all frail; consider none more frail than yourself.

(b) On Reading the Holy Scriptures

In the Holy Scriptures, truth is to be looked for rather than fair phrases. All sacred scriptures should be read in the spirit in which they were written. In them, therefore, we should seek food for our souls rather than subtleties of speech, and we should as readily read simple and
35 devout books as those that are lofty and profound. Do not be influenced by the importance of the writer, and whether his learning be great or small, but let the love of pure truth draw you to read. Do not enquire, 'Who said this?' but pay attention to what is said.

Men pass away, but the word of the Lord endures for ever.
40 God speaks to us in different ways, and is no respecter of persons. But curiosity often hinders us in the reading of the Scriptures, for we try to examine and dispute over matters that we should pass over and accept in simplicity. If you desire to profit, read with humility, simplicity, and faith, and have no concern to appear learned.

Erasmus never did

(c) On the Good and Peaceful Man

45 Firstly, be peaceful yourself, and you will be able to bring peace to others. A man of peace does more good than a very learned man. A passionate man turns even good into evil, and readily listens to evil; but a good and peaceable man turns all things to good. He who is truly at peace thinks evil of no one; but he who is discontented and restless is
50 tormented by suspicions beyond number. He has no peace in himself, nor will he allow others any peace.

Thomas à Kempis, *The Imitation of Christ*, c.1441, trans. L. Sherley-Price, 1952, pp. 28–9, 32–3, 70–1

Questions

a   Thomas à Kempis is today the best known of the advocates of the *devotio moderna*, which involved concentrating on the personal religious life. How is this attitude exemplified in this extract?

★ b   Contrast the kind of life described here with (i) that of the popes and higher church dignitaries of the time and (ii) the Biblical scholars and humanists of the early sixteenth century,

c   In what ways could extract (c) be seen as a description of Luther's early struggles with his Christian faith?

7 Biblical Scholarship

When I was hunting last summer in an old library – for no coverts afford more delightful sport – some game of no common sort fell unexpectedly into my nets. It was Laurentius Valla's Notes on the New Testament. . . I imagine there will be some persons, who as soon as they
5 read the title of the work, and before they know anything of its contents, will exclaim loudly against it; and that the most odious outcry will be raised by those who will chiefly benefit by the publication, I mean the theologians . . . [yet] what crime is it in Laurentius, if after collating some ancient and correct Greek copies, he has noted in the
10 New Testament, which is derived from the Greek, some passages which either differ from our version, or seem to be inaptly rendered owing to a passing want of vigilance in the translator, or are expressed more significantly in the Greek; or finally if it appears that something in our text is corrupt? . . .
15 If they reply that Theology is too great to be confined by the laws of Grammar, and that all this work of interpretation depends upon the influence of the Holy Spirit, it is truly a new dignity for divines, if they are the only people who are privileged to speak incorrectly. But let them explain first what Jerome means when he writes to Desiderius
20 [Erasmus]: It is one thing to be a prophet and another to be an interpreter; in one case the Spirit foretells future events, in the other sentences are understood and translated by erudition and command of language. Again, what is the use of Jerome laying down rules for the translation of the sacred writings, if that faculty comes by inspiration?
25 Lastly, why is Paul said to be more eloquent in Hebrew than in Greek? And if it was possible for the interpreters of the Old Testament to make some mistakes, especially in matters not affecting the faith, why may it not be the same with the New, of which Jerome did not so much make a translation as emend an old one, and that not strictly, leaving words, as
30 he himself testifies, some of which are those principally called in question by Laurentius? Again, shall we ascribe to the Holy Spirit the errors which we ourselves make? Suppose the interpreters translated rightly, still what has been rightly translated may be perverted. Jerome emended, but what he emended is now again corrupted; unless it can be
35 asserted that there is now less presumption among the half-learned, or more skill in languages, and not rather corruption made easier than ever by printing, which propagates a single error in a thousand copies at once. . .
And if there are any who have not the leisure to learn Greek
40 thoroughly, they may still obtain no small help by the studies of Valla, who has examined with remarkable sagacity the whole New Testament. . . I conclude that the studious will owe much to Laurentius, and Laurentius will owe much to you, through whom he is presented to the public, and by whose judgment and patronage he will be more

45   commended to good intellects, and better protected against the
malevolent.

Erasmus to Christopher Fish, March 1505, in R. L. DeMolen,
Erasmus: Documents of Modern History, 1973, pp. 59–62

Questions

★ *a*   Who was Jerome (line 19) and for what great work was he
responsible?

   b   What does the extract say was the purpose of Valla's work? Why
had this purpose been criticised?

   c   Why was 'corruption made easier than ever by printing' (lines 36–
7)?

★ *d*   In what ways did Erasmus himself subsequently continue and
develop the work of Valla as described here?

8   From 'In Praise of Folly'

Folly speaks:
But there's no doubt that those folk are all men of my kidney who
delight in miracles and fictitious marvels, whether hearing or telling
about them. . . .

5   Closely related to them are the people who've adopted the foolish but
pleasurable belief that if they see some carving or painting of that
towering Polyphemus, Christopher, they're sure not to die that day, or
if anyone addresses a statue of Barbara in the set formula he'll return
unhurt from battle. . .The ordinary life of Christians everywhere
10   abounds in these varieties of silliness, and they are readily permitted and
encouraged by priests who are not unaware of the profit to be made
thereby. Meanwhile, if some disagreeable wiseacre were to get up and
interrupt with a statement of the true facts: 'You won't do badly when
you die if you've been good in your lifetime. You'll redeem your sins
15   only by adding hatred for wrongdoing, tears, vigils, prayers, fasts, and a
change in your whole way of living to the small sum you've already
paid. The saint will protect you if you'll try to imitate his life' – if, I
repeat, your wise man starts blurting out these uncomfortable truths,
you can see how he'll soon destroy the world's peace of mind and
20   plunge it into confusion. . . .
        Then the Supreme Pontiffs, who are the vicars of Christ: if they made
an attempt to imitate his life of poverty and toil, his teaching, cross, and
contempt for life, and thought about their name of Pope, which means
Father, or their title of Supreme Holiness, what creature on earth would
25   be so cast down? . . . But as things are today, any work that has to be
done they can leave to Peter and Paul, who have plenty of time on their
hands, while claiming all the pomp and pleasure for themselves.
Consequently, and again, thanks to me, practically no class of man lives
so comfortably with fewer cares; for they believe they do quite enough

30   for Christ if they play their part as overseer by means of every kind of
ritual, near-theatrical ceremonial and display, benedictions and
anathemas, and all their titles of Your Beatitude, Reverence, and
Holiness. For them it's out-of-date and outmoded to perform miracles;
teaching the people is too like hard work, interpreting the holy
35   scriptures is for schoolmen, and praying is a waste of time; to shed tears
is weak and womanish, to be needy is degrading; to suffer defeat is a
disgrace and hardly fitting for one who scarcely permits the greatest of
kings to kiss the toes of his sacred feet; and finally, death is an
unattractive prospect, and dying on a cross would be an ignominious
40   end.

Erasmus, *In Praise of Folly, 1509*, trans. Betty Radice, 1971,
pp. 125–6, 130, 178–80

Questions

a   What 'varieties of silliness' (line 10) is Erasmus attacking?
b   Why does he say that the 'true facts' are 'uncomfortable truths' (line 18)?
c   In what ways does he suggest that the popes are not behaving as they should?
★ *d*   Why would Luther have agreed with Erasmus on this subject?
e   'In Praise of Folly' was written to amuse Thomas More. On the evidence of this extract, do you think Erasmus is likely to have been successful?

9 An Attack on the Church

From *Die Totenfresser*, a dramatic poem about those who feed upon the dead

[From a speech by the pope]

  Be quiet about the gospel
  And preach only papal law.
  We will then be lords and the laity servants
  Who bear the burdens we lay upon them.
5   All is lost however
  If the gospel gets out
  And things are measured by it.
  For it teaches none to give and sacrifice to us –
  Only that we should live simple, impoverished lives. . . .
10   Church offerings, weekly, monthly, and annual masses for the dead
  Bring us more than enough.
  Pity the hardship it inflicts upon the children of the givers!
  But if we will now just take care
  We can remain free and secure
15   In no way bound to any layman
  Neither by tolls, taxes, or other burdens.
  We owe only holy water, salt, and three hazel nuts!

On earth none have it better than us.
Indulgences lend a hand
20 By making men fearful of penance.
We also put a lot of stock in purgatory
(Although Scripture doesn't have much to say about it).
The reason is that we must use every chance
To scare the hell out of common folk.
25 For that is what keeps the cover on our deception.
So if you want to continue
In your comfort and mischief
I will help you with my laws
So that no one dare oppose you.
30 You may steal and strike whom you please
And no layman will dare lay a hand on you –
So long as we keep up our pretences!
So let us plague and punish the world
For wine, grain, meat, and cash
35 And be thankful to the dead
Who make it possible for us to fleece the living.

> Nicholas Manuel, 1521, in Steven E. Ozment, *The Reformation in the Cities*, 1975, pp. 112–13

Questions

a In what ways does the pope suggest that the clergy should 'scare the hell out of common folk' (line 24)?

b What reason does he give for doing this?

c What criticisms of the church is the author in fact making? In what ways do other extracts in this section support these criticisms?

10   The Sale of Indulgences

(a) The Pope authorises the sale of indulgences

Our aim is that the salvation of souls may be secured above all at that time when they most need the intercessions of others and are least able to help themselves. We wish by our Apostolic authority to draw on the treasury of the Church and to succour the souls in purgatory who died
5 united with Christ through love and whose lives have merited that such intercessions should now be offered through an Indulgence of this kind.

With the longings of such great paternal affection as with God's help we can achieve, in reliance on the divine mercy and the plenitude of our power, we grant by concession and indulgence as follows:

10 If any parents, friends or other Christians are moved by obligations of piety towards these very souls who are exposed to the fire of purgatory for the expiation of punishments which by divine justice are their due:

Let them during the stated period of ten years give a fixed amount
or value of money, as laid down by its dean and chapter or by our
own collector, for the repair of the church of Saints, paying either in
person at the Church or by duly accredited messenger:

It is then our will that plenary remission should avail by
intercession for the said souls in purgatory, to win them relief from
their punishments – the souls, that is, for whose sakes the stated
quantity or value of money has been paid in the manner declared.

From the Bull 'Salvator Noster' of Pope Sixtus IV, 3 August 1476,
in E. G. Rupp and B. Drewery, *Luther: Documents of Modern
History*, 1970, pp. 15–17

(b) The 'Instructio Summaria' of Albert of Mainz, 1515

The following are the four principal gifts of grace that have been
granted by the Apostolic Bull: any one of them can be had separately. It
is on these four Indulgences that the preachers must concentrate their
utmost diligence, infiltrating them one by one into the ears of the
faithful in the most effective way, and explaining them with all the
ability they have.

The first principal grace is the plenary remission of all sins . . . .

The second principal grace is the confessional . . . .

The third principal grace is participation in all the blessings of the
universal Church . . . .

The fourth principal grace is the plenary remission of all sins for the
souls that exist in purgatory, which the Pope grants and concedes by
means of intercessions, so that a contribution placed by the living in the
repository on their behalf counts as one which a man might make or
give for himself. . . .

There is no need for the contributors to be of contrite heart or to
make oral confession, since this grace depends (as the Bull makes clear)
on the love in which the departed died and the contributions which the
living pay.

E. G. Rupp and B. Drewery, *Luther: Documents of Modern History*,
1970, pp. 15–17

Questions

★ *a*   What did the church teach was the purpose of purgatory (line 4)?
How could 'parents, friends or other Christians' (line 10) help souls
in purgatory?

   b   What was the pope's purpose in issuing this bull?

   c   What does the bull say that the money raised by the sale of
indulgences was to be used for? In what ways might this intention
be criticised?

★ *d*   What offices were held by Albert of Mainz when he issued his
'instruction'? Why did he need the money to be raised by the sale of
indulgences?

e   In what significant way did this 'instruction' explicitly go beyond what Sixtus IV had authorised in his bull?

f   How was this 'instruction' exploited by those, such as Tetzel, who sold indulgences? Why did they rouse Luther's wrath?

II Martin Luther: Personal and Political

The main outlines of Luther's career are very well known, but it is not always appreciated how short a period, less than ten years, was occupied by all the main events of Luther's life. His early years and his education, especially his wrestlings with Christian doctrine in the monastery and in his lectures at Wittenberg, were the necessary preliminaries to his emergence on the German scene with his attack on indulgences in 1517 (see Chapter III). This was quite quickly followed by various disputations with leading churchmen, the publication of several other works (also considered in Chapter III) and his excommunication and confrontation with the Emperor at Worms. Following his year in hiding, Luther returned to Wittenberg, got married in 1523 and then, despite his notoriety in Germany, settled down and spent the rest of his life as a university teacher.

It is difficult to separate completely Luther's political activities and writings from his theological work, and it is a rather artificial division, but for convenience the attempt has been made here. Clearly the appearance at Worms was a 'political' event of the first importance – and for other views of it see Chapter VII extract 3 and Chapter VIII extract 3. Apart from this, Luther did not really take any active role in politics but his opinion was frequently sought on all kinds of issues.

The peasants' revolt was the most important of these. The peasants' articles, explaining the reasons for their revolt, appealed to Luther's teachings, particularly his doctrine of the priesthood of all believers, as one of the justifications for their action and so some reply from Luther was obviously called for. His views on a Christian's civic responsibilities meant inevitably that he could not support the peasants, although his first response to them was noticeably less severe than his second, which damaged his reputation among the peasants as a whole, not just those who had rebelled.

Another political problem was the Lutherans' relationship with the Roman Catholic church. Luther believed by the end of his life that it had been permanently undermined, at least in Germany, but he also saw the necessity for a general council of the church to help solve the problems of both church and society. Obviously Luther did not foresee the actual meeting and decisions of the Council of Trent, which opened only a short time before his death and which ultimately led to some retreat of the Lutheran church in Germany, but he did realise that something needed to be done.

1 Early Life

(a) When he was old enough to be taught, his parents accustomed the boy Martin, by diligent instruction at home, to the knowledge and fear of God and to the duties of the other virtues; and as is usual with honourable people, they took care that he should learn to read. . . . He
5 next attended school in Eisenach for four years, where he heard his teacher present grammar more correctly and skilfully than he had heard it presented elsewhere. I remember hearing Luther praise this man's talent. But the reason that he was sent to Eisenach was that his mother had been born in those parts, of an old and respected family. . . .
10   Having thus tasted the delights of literature, and aflame with a natural greed for learning, he aspired to the university as to the fount of all teaching. And such brilliance could well have grasped all the arts in order if only he had found suitable teachers, and perhaps the gentler studies of true philosophy and a concern for polished discourse might
15 have served to relieve the vehemence of his nature. But at Erfurt . . . his penetrating intellect enabled him to grasp arguments and fundamental precepts better than others. His mind was avid for teaching and kept on demanding more and better things, so on his own he read most of the collections of ancient Latin writers, Cicero, Virgil, Livy and others. . . .
20 He examined the opinions and advice of these writers more clearly, and as he had an accurate and retentive memory, most of what he heard read to him remained in his mind and before his eyes. . . . At the age of twenty, acting on the advice of his kinsfolk who believed that cleverness and eloquence as great as his should be brought out into the open and
25 into public affairs, he began the study of law.

(b) A little later when he was twenty-one years old, against the advice of his parents and friends, he suddenly went to the cloister of the Augustinian monks at Erfurt, and asked to be received. After he was received, he not only studied the doctrine of the Church most zealously,
30 but also subjected himself to the severest discipline, far surpassing everyone in the appointed reading, disputation, fasting, and prayer. . . . It was not poverty, but the desire for godliness, which led him into the monastic life.

From Philip Melanchthon's life of Luther, 1546, in I. D. K. Siggins (ed.), *Luther*, 1972, pp. 32–4

(c) I was very holy under the papacy: I was a monk! And yet I was so
35 sad and depressed that I thought that God was not gracious to me. There I celebrated mass, and I prayed, and I had no wife – you never saw or experienced such a member of an order or monk as I was (so to speak). Nowadays, I must suffer other thoughts from the devil. For he often casts in my teeth: 'Oh, what a huge crowd of people you have led astray
40 with your teaching!' Sometimes in the midst of trial a harsh word comforts me and gives me new heart. On one occasion, my father

confessor said to me when I was constantly bringing stupid sins to him: 'You are a fool! God does not rage at you, but you rage at him; God is not angry with you, but you are angry with him!'

Martin Luther's Table Talk, 1531, I. D. K. Siggins (ed.), *Luther*, 1972, p. 43

Questions

★ *a* How does Melanchthon think the 'vehemence' of Luther's 'nature' could have been 'relieved' (line 15)? What evidence can you find from the rest of Luther's career to illustrate this 'vehemence'?

★ *b* What reason, apart from those given in the text, was there for urging a clever boy like Luther to study law?

c What kind of monk was Luther, according to these extracts? Why did he find monastic life so difficult?

d What does Luther mean when he says the devil tells him he has 'led astray' with his teaching a 'huge crowd of people' (line 39)?

2 Luther's 'Conversion'

Meanwhile, in that year [1519] I had once again turned to the task of interpreting the *Psalms*, relying on the fact that I was in better training for it since I had handled in the schools the epistles of St. Paul to the Romans and Galatians, and the epistle to the Hebrews. I had certainly
5 been seized with a wondrous eagerness to understand Paul in the epistle to the Romans, but hitherto I had been held up – not by a 'lack of heart in my heart's blood', but by one word only, in chapter 1: 'The Righteousness of God is revealed in [the Gospel].' For I hated this word 'righteousness of God', which by the customary use of all the doctors I
10 had been taught to understand philosophically as what they call the *formal* or *active righteousness* whereby God is just and punishes unjust sinners.

For my case was this: however irreproachable my life as a monk, I felt myself in the presence of God to be a sinner with a most unquiet conscience, nor could I believe him to be appeased by the satisfaction I
15 could offer. I did not love – nay, I hated this just God who punishes sinners, and if not with silent blasphemy, at least with huge murmuring I was indignant against God, as it were really not enough that miserable sinners, eternally ruined by original sin, should be crushed with every kind of calamity through the law of the Ten Commandmants, but that
20 God through the Gospel must add sorrow to sorrow, and even through the Gospel bring his righteousness and wrath to bear on us. And so I raged with a savage and confounded conscience.

At last, as I meditated day and night, God showed mercy and I turned my attention to the connection of the words, namely – 'The
25 righteousness of God is revealed, as it is written: the righteous shall live by faith' – and there I began to understand that the righteousness of God is the righteousness in which a just man lives by the gift of God, in

other words by faith, and that what Paul means is this: the righteousness
of God, revealed in the Gospel, is *passive*, in other words that by which
30   the merciful God justifies us through faith, as it is written, 'The
righteous shall live by faith'. At this stage I felt myself straightway born
afresh and to have entered through the open gates into paradise itself.
There and then the whole face of scripture was changed.

> Martin Luther, *Autobiographical Fragment*, 1545, in E. G. Rupp and
> B. Drewery, *Luther: Documents of Modern History*, 1970, pp. 5–6

Questions

a   Why does Luther say that he 'raged' against God (line 22)?
b   What does Luther mean by saying that 'the righteousness of God,
      revealed in the Gospel, is passive' (lines 28–9)? How important was
      his appointment to Wittenburg University to this revelation?
★ *c*   What effect did this understanding have on Luther's life and
      teaching?

3 How Martin Luther Met Me on the Road to Wittenberg, 1522

And here I cannot omit, though it may sound trivial and even childish
to tell how Martin, on his way from his confinement back to
Wittenberg, met me and my companion. As we made our way to
Wittenberg, for the sake of studying holy scripture we came to
5   Jena . . . . At the town gate we met a respectable man who . . . showed
us this inn just outside the town. The landlord came to the door . . . and
led us into the parlour. Here we found one man, all by himself at a table
with a book propped in front of him. He greeted us kindly and
beckoned us to sit at this table. . . . Then he drank our health, which we
10   could not refuse, and so reassured by his friendliness and neighbourliness
we sat down at the table to which he had bidden us and ordered some
wine, that we might return his toast.
      We took him for a knight, as he sat there, dressed after the fashion of
that country, with a red hood, plain doublet and hose, a sword at his
15   side, his right hand on its hilt, the other on his book. Then he asked
where we came from [and] we asked, 'Sir, can you tell us whether Dr
Martin Luther is in Wittenberg just now, or where else he may be?' He
replied 'I know for certain that he is not in Wittenberg at this moment.
But Philip Melanchthon is there and he teaches Greek and others teach
20   Hebrew.' And he advised us strongly to study these two languages. . . .
      'My boys,' he asked, 'what do they think about this Luther in
Switzerland?' 'Sir, there are many different opinions. Some cannot extol
him too highly and thank God for revealing truth and confounding
error through him, but others revile him as an unconscionable heretic,
25   especially the clergy.' He said, 'That I understand – those parsons!' . . .

The landlord went out of the door and after a little beckoned me to him and said, 'Because you have such a sincere desire to see Martin Luther – there he is sitting next to you.' I thought he was having me on, and said, 'You're joking because you know how much I long to see
30   him.' He said, 'It's the truth, but don't let on that you know who he is.' . . .

During dinner Martin kept up edifying and friendly conversation, so that . . . we thought more about his words than about the food. Among other things he complained with sighing how at this time the German
35   princes and nobles were assembled in Diet in Nuremberg, on account of God's Word, and the ups and downs and grievances of the affairs of the German nation, but were only concerned to have a good time . . . instead of coming before God with fear and earnest prayer. 'But there's your Christian princes for you!'

John Kessler, *Sabbata*, in E. G. Rupp and B. Drewery, *Luther: Documents of Modern History*, 1970, pp. 82–5

Questions

a   Where had Luther been in 'confinement' (line 2) and why could he be taken 'for a knight' (line 13)?
b   Why did Luther advocate the study of Greek and Hebrew?
c   Why was it 'especially the clergy' (line 25) who reviled Luther?
★   d   What was the Diet (line 35) and why was it meeting in Nuremberg at this time?
e   What characteristics of Luther does this extract illustrate and how does the picture of him here compare with his character as shown in other extracts in this chapter?

4   Luther's Marriage

(a) Those nine apostate nuns have come to me. They are a wretched crowd, but they were conducted here by some upright citizens of Torgau . . . so there are no grounds for unjust suspicion. . . You ask what I shall do with them? First I shall indicate to their families that they should
5   support them. If they will not, I shall take care that they are looked after elsewhere, for people have promised me to help. I shall also arrange marriages for some of them, where I can.

Luther to George Spalatin, 1523

(b) Grace and peace in the Lord! . . . Indeed the story is true that I have suddenly been married to Katherine, before I had to listen to people
10   mouthing tirades against me as usually happens. For I hope that I may stay alive for a short time yet, and I was unwilling to deny my father, who entreated this last obedience, his hope for descendants, and at the same time to confirm in deed what I have taught in words, since I

discover that so many people are timid even in the great light of the
15 gospel. Thus God wished and God acted. For I am not in love, nor do I
burn with desire; but I cherish my wife. Next Tuesday, therefore I shall
give a feast in celebration of my marriage, at which my parents will be
present.

     Luther to Nicholas von Amsdorf, 1525

(c) I would not exchange my Katie for France or for Venice: first,
20 because God has given her to me and has given me to her; secondly,
because I have often discovered that there are more faults in other
women than in my Katie (even though she has some too, they are
counterbalanced by many great virtues); thirdly, because she preserves
the faith of marriage, that is, loyalty and honour.

     Luther's Table Talk, 1531, in I. D. K. Siggins (ed.), *Luther*, 1972,
     pp. 153–5

Questions

a   Why should the 'apostate nuns' (line 1) come to Luther? What did
    he hope would happen to them?
b   What reasons for his marriage does Luther give Amsdorf? Why did
    he choose Katherine von Bora?
c   How had his attitude to Katherine at the time of their marriage
    changed by 1531?

5 Luther's Answer before the Emperor and the Diet of Worms, 18 April 1517

On the next day, the fifth of the Festival, just after four p.m., the herald
came and led Dr Martin to the imperial court. . . . When the assembly
began and Martin stood forward, the official broke out with these
words: 'Yesterday evening His Imperial Majesty prescribed this hour for
5 you, Martin Luther, when you had publicly acknowledged as your own
the books which we yesterday read out by name. But when you were
asked if you wished any of them to be withdrawn, or whether you
stood by all that you had published, you asked for time to think it over.
This time is now at an end – and indeed by rights you should not have
10 been granted any more time for consideration, for you have known
long enough why you have been summoned here.

    'Indeed, every man ought to be sure enough about his religious
beliefs to be able to give a confident and trustworthy account of them
whenever it is demanded, especially a man like you – so great and so
15 experienced a Professor of Theology. Come now: answer at last His
Majesty's question – you have appreciated his kindness in obtaining for
yourself time for reflection: do you wish to stand by the books
recognized as yours? Or do you wish to retract anything?'

The official had spoken in Latin and German, and Dr Martin replied in the same two languages speaking like a suppliant, yet without raising his voice – modestly, with no lack of Christian warmth and firmness, which whetted their appetites for the speech of his antagonist and the sight of his own high spirit humbled. Above all they looked most eagerly for his revocation, some hope of which they had conceived from his request for time for deliberation. This is what he said:

'My lord, emperor most serene, princes most illustrious, lords most gracious, I am here obedient to the order made yesterday evening that I should appear at this time. . . . Two questions were put to me yesterday by your Highness, whether I acknowledge as mine a list of books published under my name, and whether I wished to hold to my defence of them or to revoke them. I gave a deliberate and plain answer to the first, and I stand by it and always shall – namely, that the books were mine. . . .

'However, because I am a man and not God, I can bring no other protection to my writings than my Lord Jesus Christ brought to his own teaching . . . . If the Lord himself, who knew he could not err, did not disdain to listen to testimony against his teaching, even from the meanest of slaves, how much more should I, the dregs of a man, who cannot but err, seek and await for someone to bear witness against my teaching? I therefore beg by the mercy of God that your serene Majesty, your illustrious lordships, or anyone at all, from the highest to the lowest, who is able, should bear witness, convict me of error, vanquish me by the prophets or the evangelists of scripture. . . .'

To these words the imperial orator replied in tones of reproach that Luther's answer was not to the point. . . . He therefore demanded a simple answer with no strings attached: would Luther revoke or would he not?

Luther replied: 'Since your serene Majesty and your lordships request a simple answer, I shall give it, with no strings and no catches. Unless I am convicted by the testimony of scripture or plain reason (for I believe neither in Pope nor councils alone, since it is agreed that they have often erred and contradicted themselves), I am bound by the scriptures I have quoted, and my conscience is captive to the Word of God. I neither can nor will revoke anything, for it is neither safe nor honest to act against one's conscience. Amen.'

E. G. Rupp and B. Drewery, *Luther: Documents of Modern History*, 1970, pp. 58–60

Questions

★ *a* Why had Luther been summoned to Worms and what guarantee for his attendance had the Emperor given?

   b Why did 'the official' think Luther should not have had time for reflection?

c   Why did the people present at the Diet expect Luther to retract what he had written?

d   Why might the description of Luther speaking 'like a suppliant' and 'modestly' (lines 19–20) be considered rather unexpected?

e   What are the only grounds on which Luther says he is willing to be 'convicted' (line 50)? Why will he accept no others?

6   To the Elector Frederick of Saxony, 5 March 1522

To the serene high-born Prince Frederick Elector of Saxony, etc. Grace and peace! Most gracious Lord, Your Electoral Grace's writing and kind remembrance reached me on Friday evening, the night before I began my journey. That your Electoral Highness had the best intentions
5   towards me is manifest. And this is my answer. Most gracious lord, I herewith desire to make it known that I have not received the Gospel from men, but from heaven, through our Lord Jesus Christ, so that I may well (which I shall henceforth do) glory in being able to style myself a servant and evangelist. That I desired to be cited before a
10   human tribunal to have my cause tried was not because I had any doubts as to its truth, but solely because I wished to allure others. But now that I see my great humility only serves to abase the Gospel, and that Satan is ready to occupy the place I vacate, even if it be only by a hand-breadth, my conscience compels me to act differently. I have done sufficient for
15   your Grace this year in remaining in my forced seclusion. For the devil knows it was not done out of fear. He saw into my heart, when I came to Worms, that although I had known there were as many devils ready to spring upon me as there were tiles on the house-roofs, I would joyfully have sprung into their midst. . . .
20   I write all this to let your Grace see that I come to Wittenberg under higher protection than that of the Elector, and I have not the slightest intention of asking your Electoral Highness's help. For I consider I am more able to protect your Grace than you are to protect me; and, what is more, if I knew that your gracious Highness could and would protect
25   me I would not come.

    In this matter God alone must manage without any human intervention. Therefore he whose faith is greatest will receive the most protection. So, as I see your faith is very weak, I cannot regard you as the man who could either protect or save me. . . . Therefore, seeing I
30   decline to follow your Grace, then you are innocent in God's sight if I am taken prisoner or killed. Your Electoral Highness shall henceforth act thus regarding your duty towards me as Elector. You must render obedience to the powers that be, and sustain the authority of His Imperial Majesty with all your might, as is only seemly for a member of
35   the Empire, and not oppose the authorities in the event of their imprisoning or slaying me. For no one must oppose the authorities except He who has instituted them; for it is rebellion against God.

E. G. Rupp and B. Drewery, *Luther: Documents of Modern History*, 1970, pp. 80–1

Questions

★   *a*   Why had Luther been in 'forced seclusion' (line 15)? What was this to do with the Elector of Saxony?

     b   What reason does Luther give for his attendance at the 'human tribunal' (line 10) of Worms? Why has he now changed his mind about this?

     c   Why does Luther say 'I see your faith is very weak' (line 28)?

     d   Why should it be 'rebellion against God' (line 37) for the Elector to protect Luther? In what way does it appear that Luther is not proposing to follow his own advice?

7 Luther's Replies to the Peasants
(a) An Admonition to Peace, 1524

The peasants who have now banded together in Swabia have put their intolerable grievances against the rulers into twelve articles, and undertaken to support them with certain passages of Scripture, and have published them in printed form. The thing about them that pleases
5   me best is that, in the twelfth article, they . . . are willing to be corrected, in so far as that can be done by clear, plain and undeniable passages of Scripture. . . .

     To the Princes and Lords. We have no one on earth to thank for this mischievous rebellion, except you princes and lords; and especially you
10   blind bishops and mad priests and monks, whose hearts are hardened, even to the present day, and who do not cease to rage against the holy Gospel. . . Besides, in your temporal government, you do nothing but flay and rob your subjects, in order that you may lead a life of splendor and pride, until the poor common people can bear it no longer. . . .
15   To the peasants. So far, dear friends, you have learned only that I admit it to be (sad to say!) all too true and certain that the princes and lords, who forbid the preaching of the Gospel and oppress the people so unbearably, are worthy, and have well deserved, that God put them down from their seats, as men who have sinned deeply against God and
20   man. . . . Nevertheless, you, too, must have a care that you take up your cause with a good conscience and with justice. . . .

     If your enterprise were right, then any man might become judge over another, and there would remain in the world neither authority nor government, nor order, nor land, but there would be only murder and
25   bloodshed; for as soon as anyone saw that someone was wronging him, he would turn to and judge him and punish him. Now if that is unjust and intolerable when done by an individual, neither can it be endured when done by a band or a crowd. And what would you do yourselves,

if disorder broke out in your band,
30   another and took his own vengeance

(b) Against the Robbing and Mur

In the former book I did not ventu
had offered to be set right and
command . . . says that we are not
they go on, and, forgetting their
35   violence, and rob and rage and act li
what they had in their false minds
made in their twelve articles, un
nothing but lies. . . .

The peasants have taken on the
40   sins against God and man, by which they
death in body and soul. In the first place they have sworn to be true and
faithful, submissive and obedient, to their rulers. . . Because they are
breaking this obedience, and are setting themselves against the high
powers, wilfully and with violence, they have forfeited body and
45   soul. . . .

In the second place, they are starting a rebellion, and violently
robbing and plundering monasteries and castles which are not theirs, by
which they have a second time deserved death in body and soul. . . .

In the third place, they cloak this terrible and horrible sin with the
50   Gospel, call themselves 'Christian brethren', receive oaths and homage,
and compel people to hold with them to these abominations. Thus they
become the greatest of all blasphemers of God and slanderers of His holy
Name, serving the devil, under the outward appearance of the Gospel,
thus earning death in body and soul ten times over.

> Martin Luther, May 1525, in K. C. Sessions, *Reformation and
> Authority*, 1968, pp. 29–33, 38–9

Questions

  a On what grounds does Luther at first apparently approve of what
the peasants were demanding?
  b Why does Luther caution the peasants to 'have a care' (line 20)?
  c Why had Luther changed his mind about the peasants' actions by
the time he wrote the tract from which extract **(b)** comes?
  d Why does he particularly attack the fact that the peasants call
themselves 'Christian brethren' (line 50)?
★ *e* What effect did the publication of this tract have on Luther's
reputation and support in Germany?

8 The Christian and Temporal Authority

(a) We must firmly establish secular law and the sword, that no one
may doubt that it is in the world by God's will and ordinance. . . .

We must divide all the children of Adam into two classes; the first belong to the kingdom of God, the second to the kingdom of the world. Those belonging to the kingdom of God are all true believers in Christ and are subject to Christ. . . . Now observe, these people need no secular sword or law. And if all the world were composed of real Christians, that is, true believers, no prince, king, lord, sword, or law would be needed. For what were the use of them, since Christians have in their hearts the Holy Spirit, who instructs them and causes them to wrong no one, to love every one, willingly and cheerfully to suffer injustice and even death from every one. . . .

Since, however, a true Christian lives and labors on earth not for himself, but for his neighbor, therefore the whole spirit of his life impels him to do even that which he need not do, but which is profitable and necessary for his neighbor. Because the sword is a very great benefit and necessary to the whole world, to preserve peace, to punish sin and to prevent evil, he submits most willingly to the rule of the sword, pays taxes, honors those in authority, serves, helps, and does all he can to further the government, that it may be sustained and held in honor and fear. . . .

A prince's duty is fourfold: First, that toward God consists in true confidence and in sincere prayer; second, that toward his subjects consists in love and Christian service; third, that toward his counselors and rulers consists in an open mind and unfettered judgment; fourth, that toward evil doers consists in proper zeal and firmness. Then his state is right, outwardly and inwardly, pleasing to God and to the people.

Martin Luther, *Secular Authority: To What Extent It Should Be Obeyed*, 1522, in K. C. Sessions (ed.), *Reformation and Authority*, 1968, pp. 25–8

(b) You may ask: 'Should a prince not engage in war? Should his subjects not follow him into battle?' . . . To answer briefly: to act in a Christian manner, I say, no prince should make war against his overlord. . . However, if your opponent is your equal, or inferior to you, or a foreign government, first of all you should offer him justice and peace. . . . If he refuses, then consider your own best interests and protect yourself with force against force. . . . And in so doing you must pay attention to your subjects to whom you are responsible for protection and aid, in order that such tasks may be done in love. . . .

In this task subjects are duty bound to obey, staking their life and property upon it. For in this situation one must wager his goods and his own self for the sake of others. In such a war it is both Christian and a work of love courageously to slay, rob, and burn the enemy. . . .

If the prince is not in the right, is his people still duty bound to follow him? Answer: No. For no one ought to act against the right, but one must obey God (who wants the right to prevail) more than men.

Martin Luther, *On Temporal Authority*, 1523, in I. D. K. Siggins (ed.), *Luther*, 1972, pp. 144–5

9   A General Council is Needed

Since the pope, Paul III by name, last year recorded his intention of holding a council at Whitsuntide in Mantua, and then transferred it from Mantua so that no one knows where he will or can hold it; and since we for our part have to anticipate that we shall either be
5   summoned to the council or else condemned unsummoned, I was commanded to draw up and collect the articles of our doctrine in case negotiations arose about where, and how far, we would or could make concessions to the papists, and on what points we determined to persist and persevere to the end.
10   Accordingly, I have compiled these articles and presented them to our side. They have also been accepted by our side, and unanimously confessed and agreed upon, so that if the Pope and his side should one day become so bold as to hold a genuinely free council, without lying and trickery, earnestly and truthfully as his duty requires, these articles
15   should be presented publicly and set out as the confession of our faith. But the Romish court is horribly afraid of a free council, and shuns the light so shamefully that even its own adherents have been robbed of hope that it will ever again permit a free council, much less hold one itself. (For they are quite properly very distressed at this and have no
20   little ground for complaint, since it leads them to think that the Pope would rather see the whole of Christendom lost and all souls condemned before he would be willing to reform himself or his party a little, and have his tyranny somewhat limited.). . .
        I would really and truly like to see a genuine council: many matters
25   and many people would be helped by it. Not that we need it, for our churches are now, through God's grace, so illumined and supplied by the pure Word and the right use of the sacrament, with understanding of the various callings and just works, that we on our part ask for no council and on these issues think nothing better can be hoped for or

30   expected from a council. But in bishoprics everywhere we see so many parishes vacant and deserted that one's heart would break. . .

    In addition to such urgent church affairs, there are also countless matters of great importance needing improvement in the secular realm, such as the discord between the princes and the estates; usury and
35   rapacity have burst in like a flood and have become quite lawful . . . and all kinds of vice and depravity, disobedience on the part of subjects, servants, and labourers, dishonesty in all the crafts and among the peasants − who can reckon it all? − have got so far out of hand that one could not bring them back to rights with ten councils and twenty diets.
40   If a council were to take up these vital matters which oppose God in the spiritual and secular realms, everyone would find their hands so full of things to do that for the time being they could well forget their childish games.

        Martin Luther, Preface to his *Schmalkald Articles*, 1538, in I. D. K. Siggins (ed.), Luther, 1972, pp. 140–2

Questions

★   *a*   This document was commissioned by the Schmalkaldic League. Who had formed the League and why did Luther describe it as 'our side' (lines 10–11)?

★   *b*   What did Luther mean by a 'genuinely free council' (line 13)? Why was the pope so reluctant to hold a council? What reason does Luther give for this reluctance?

     c   What was 'usury' and why was it not considered to be 'lawful' (lines 34–5)? What grounds were there for regarding this and the other social problems mentioned in this paragraph as matters for consideration by a church council?

     d   Luther appears to have regarded himself as both still part of the Roman Catholic Church and as not subject to the pope's jurisdiction. What evidence is there of both these attitudes in this extract?

10   Education

'Well,' you say, 'everyone is perfectly able to teach his daughters and sons himself, or to train them with discipline.' Answer: Yes, indeed, it is obvious how such teaching and training work! Even when discipline is applied most rigorously and turns out well, it achieves nothing more
5   than a forced little air of respectability; otherwise they remain just the same utter blockheads who do not know how to distinguish this from that and are unable to give help or advice to anyone. But if they were taught and trained in schools or other places, there would be learned and qualified masters and mistresses, the languages and other arts and history
10   would be taught, they would hear of the doings and sayings of the

whole world, what happened to various cities, kingdoms, princes, men and women, and thus in a short time could set before themselves, as in a mirror, the nature, life, advice and values, successes and failures of the whole world from the beginning. From this they could then improve their minds and conduct themselves in the course of their lives in the fear of God, and from the same histories become sensitive and prudent about what to seek and what to avoid in this outward life, and then also advise and direct others. But training undertaken at home without such schools tries to make us wise through our own experience. . . . For myself, I say: If I had children and could do it, I would see to it that they not only studied language and history, but also learned singing and music and the whole of mathematics.

> Martin Luther, 1524, in ed. I. D. K. Siggins, *Luther*, 1972, pp. 146–7

Questions

a   What are the advantages for children of going to school rather than being taught at home?

b   Do you agree with Luther that it is not a good idea to try 'to make us wise through our own experience' (line 19)?

c   Why does Luther regard the study of history as so important? Does your own education lead you to agree?

★   d   How does the ideal education advocated in this extract compare with Luther's own education, as described in extract 1 above?

III   Martin Luther: Theology

Theology was not directly the cause of Luther's quarrel with the papacy, but it was the chief reason why a reconciliation was impossible. Luther developed his theological ideas while expounding in particular Paul's Epistle to the Romans, at Wittenberg University. However, he might have remained a relatively obscure university teacher had it not been for the indulgence controversy and the fame this generated for him.

Justification by faith and the priesthood of all believers proved to be revolutionary ideas. Luther introduced the notion of God offering grace to each individual, who had only to decide to accept it; at a stroke he thus stressed the responsibility of each individual for his own salvation and undermined the work of the church, based on the need to earn one's place in heaven, through the sacraments above all, and eliminated the fear of purgatory and the need for indulgences.

The priesthood of all believers was another extremely powerful idea, which had political as well as religious implications, such as providing the grounds for the appeal to Luther of some rebellious peasants in 1524–5 for support against their lords. Unfortunately for them, Luther only interpreted the idea in a religious sense and not as absolving citizens from their allegiance to their God-given rulers. Nevertheless it did damage the mystique of the priesthood, suggesting that priests were no different from other men, thus for example allowing the clergy to marry, but also lowering their social standing.

The combination of these ideas with Luther's doctrine of the 'real presence' in the elements at communion and his stress on understanding the Bible was totally unacceptable to the Roman church. To understand why, it is necessary to appreciate not only the force of Luther's teaching but to be able to compare it with what was taught by Zwingli and Calvin as well as the Anabaptists and the Roman Catholics; these different faiths all sought the exclusive allegiance of their followers so that the divisions between them became increasingly impossible to bridge.

1   A Sermon on Indulgences

Even if indulgences are the very merit of Christ and his saints and are therefore to be received with all reverence, in practice they have become the most disgraceful agency of avarice. For is anyone using them to seek the salvation of men's souls, rather than the cash out of their purses? This
5 is plain and obvious from their own ministry: for the commissioners and

ministers never preach anything else but to commend indulgences and
to arouse the people to contribute. You will not hear from them who is
to teach the people, or what indulgences are, or on what day they apply
and cease to apply, but only how much they ought to contribute – in
10   other words, they leave the people hanging in their ignorance, believing
that they are immediately saved by getting these indulgences of theirs.
For the grace by which a man becomes righteous or more righteous is
not conferred by an indulgence, at least *per se*; all that is conferred is
remission of an imposed penance and satisfaction, and it does not follow
15   that a man who dies with such a remission will spring immediately to
heaven. But a simple-minded man – like the majority of the people who
have been deceived – believes that by 'plenary remission' sin is entirely
removed so that he will immediately spring to heaven, and so he sins
with impunity and binds himself even more tightly with the bonds of
20   conscience.
    . . . Remission is the relaxation of the temporal penalty one is forced
to bear here when it is imposed or to discharge the residue in purgatory
(for example, at one time seven years used to be imposed for a single
sin); but by this remission the concupiscence and sickness of the soul is in
25   no way diminished, nor is love or any other interior virtue increased,
even though all these things must happen before men enter the kingdom
of God. For flesh and blood will not possess the kingdom of God, nor
will anything defiled enter it. But how much this shortens the time in
purgatory, no one knows. Moreover, it is by no means through the
30   power of the keys that the Pope provides this remission, but only
through the application of the intercession of the entire Church. There
remains a doubt whether God will accept this in part or in whole. Of
course, the Pope is able to release a soul from purgatory when he
imposes or is able to impose the penance himself. . . . It is therefore the
35   height of temerity to preach that souls are redeemed from purgatory
through these indulgences, since the form of words is absurd, and they
do not explain how they intend them to be understood. Otherwise the
Pope is cruel, if he does not grant to souls for nothing what he is able to
grant the Church for the necessary fee.

> Martin Luther, 1516, in I. D. K. Siggins (ed.), *Luther*, 1972,
> pp. 54–5

Questions

a   What is meant by 'penance' (line 14) and 'the power of the keys'
(line 30)?
b   In what ways does Luther say that the 'commissioners and
ministers' (lines 5–6) are not doing their job properly? How does
his criticism compare with Albert of Mainz's direction about the
sale of indulgences in Chapter I extract 10 (b)?
c   Why does Luther argue that 'the Pope is cruel' (line 38) in
authorising the sale of indulgences?

★ *d*   This sermon was preached a year before Luther wrote his ninety-five theses. Why were indulgences annually a source of revenue to the Elector of Saxony and so a reason for this sermon to be preached?

2   An Attack on Indulgences

To the Right Reverend Father in Christ, Lord Albrecht, Archbishop of Magdeburg and Mainz, his esteemed lord and shepherd in Christ. May the Grace of God be with him.

5   May your Electoral Highness graciously permit me, the least and most unworthy of men, to address you . . .

With your Electoral Highness's consent, the Papal Indulgences for the rebuilding of St. Peter's in Rome is being carried through the land. I do not complain so much of the loud cry of the preacher of Indulgences, which I have not heard, but regret the false meaning which the simple

10   folk attach to it, the poor souls believing that when they have purchased such letters they have secured their salvation, also, that the moment the money jingles in the box souls are delivered from purgatory, and that all sins will be forgiven through a letter of Indulgence, even that of reviling the blessed mother of God, were any one blasphemous enough to do so.

15   And, lastly, that through these Indulgences the man is freed from all penalties! Ah, dear God! Thus are those souls which have been committed to your care, dear Father, being led in the paths of death, and for them you will be required to render an account. . .

How then can you, through false promises of Indulgences, which do

20   not promote the salvation or sanctification of their souls, lead the people into carnal security, by declaring them free from the painful consequences of their wrong-doing with which the Church was wont to punish their sins?

For deeds of piety and love are infinitely better than Indulgences, and

25   yet the bishops do not preach these so earnestly, although it is their principal duty to proclaim the love of Christ to their people. Christ has nowhere commanded Indulgences to be preached, only the Gospel.

Luther, from Wittenberg, 31 October 1517, in E. G. Rupp and B. Drewery, *Luther: Documents of Modern History* 1970, pp. 17–18

Questions

a   Why should Luther address a letter against Indulgences to Albrecht, archbishop of Mainz? Why does Luther address him as 'your Electoral Highness' (line 4)?

b   What 'false meaning' (line 9) does Luther suggest was being made by the sellers of indulgences?

c   What is meant by 'deeds of piety and love' (line 24)? What criticism of the bishops is Luther making in this paragraph?

d   Compare the tone of this extract with that of extract l above. How do you account for the difference between them?

3   Justification by Faith

An easy thing has Christian faith seemed to many, and not a few have counted it simply as one of the Christian virtues; which they do because they have never proved it by experiment nor ever tasted the power of its virtue. For to write well about it or fully to understand what has rightly
5   been written of it is impossible for those who have never tasted its spirit when oppressed by tribulations. Once, however, a man has tasted of it no matter how little, he can never have enough of writing, speaking, thinking and hearing about it. . . .

First we consider the inner man: in what manner does a man become
10   just, free and truly Christian – that is, spiritual, new and inner? It is clear that no external thing, by whatever name it may be called, can in any way conduce to Christian righteousness or liberty, any more than it can lead the way to unrighteousness or bondage. . . .

To clear the ground completely: even contemplation, meditation and
15   everything the soul can do are of no avail. One thing, and one thing only, is necessary for the Christian life, righteousness and liberty. It is the most Holy Word of God, the Gospel of Christ, as He says (John 11.25): 'I am the resurrection and the life: he that believeth in me, though he were dead, yet shall he live.' . . . Nor was Christ sent for any other office
20   than that of the Word, and the apostolical, episcopal and entire order of clergy has been called and instituted solely for the ministry of the Word . . . .

Nor can the Word of God be received and cherished by any works whatsoever but only by faith alone. Therefore it is clear that as the soul
25   needs only the Word to live and be just, so it will be justified by faith alone and not by any works. For if it could be justified by anything else, it would not need the Word, nor in consequence would need faith. . . .

Now when a man is taught his powerlessness by the commandments and is in trouble to know by what effort he may satisfy the law . . . the
30   second part of Scripture comes to the rescue, namely God's promises which declare the glory of God and say: 'If you want to fulfill the law and avoid covetousness as the law demands, believe in Christ in whom are promised you grace, righteousness, peace, freedom and all things. If you believe, you shall have; if you do not, you shall lack.' For what you
35   find impossible to do by all the works of the law, which are many and in a manner useless, you will achieve with easy speed by faith.

We are also priests for all time, which is much better than any kingship. Our priesthood fits us to appear before God, to pray for others, and to teach one another the things that are God's. This
40   constitutes priesthood, and these functions cannot be granted to any unbeliever.

Martin Luther, *The Liberty of a Christian Man*, 1520, in
G. R. Elton, *Renaissance and Reformation* 1300–1648, 1976,
pp. 176–81

Questions

a What is meant by 'the Word' (line 22) and 'works' (line 23)? What
   was the importance of making a distinction between them

b How does Luther argue that a man becomes 'just, free and truly
   Christian' (line 10)?

★ c Why was Luther's belief in justification 'by faith alone' (lines 25–6)
   a major reason for his expulsion from the Roman Catholic church?

d How does Luther downgrade the work of the clergy in both the
   third and the last paragraphs of this extract?

★ e In what sense does he mean that 'we are also priests' (line 37)? What
   name is usually given to this idea and what were the main
   implications of it for society?

4 Concerning Christian Liberty

    I first lay down these two propositions, concerning spiritual liberty
and servitude: a Christian man is the most free lord of all, and subject to
none; a Christian man is the most dutiful servant of all, and subject to
everyone. . . .

5   One thing, and one alone, is necessary for life, justification and
Christian liberty; and that is the most holy word of God, the Gospel of
Christ. . .Hence it is clear that as the soul needs the word alone for life
and justification, so it is justified by faith alone, and not by any
works. . . . That is that Christian liberty, our faith, the effect of which
10 is, not that we should be careless or lead a bad life, but that no one
should need the law or works for justification and salvation. . . .

    Nor are we only kings and the freest of all men, but also priests for
ever, a dignity far higher than kingship, because by that priesthood we
are worthy to appear before God, to pray for others, and to teach one
15 another mutually the things which are of God. . . . Here you will ask, 'If
all who are in the Church are priests, by what character are those whom
we now call priests to be distinguished from the laity?' I reply, that by
the use of these words, 'priest', 'clergy', 'spiritual person', 'ecclesiastic',
an injustice has been done, since they have been transferred from the
20 remaining body of Christians to those few who are now, by a hurtful
custom, called ecclesiastics. For holy scripture makes no distinction
between them, except that those who are now boastfully called Popes,
bishops, and lords, it calls ministers, servants, and stewards, who are to
serve the rest in the ministry of the word, for teaching the faith of Christ
25 and the liberty of believers.

    And now let us turn to the other part: to the outward man . . . . Here
then works begin; here he must not take his ease; here he must give heed

exercise his body by fastings, watchings, labour and other regular
cipline, so that it may be subdued to the spirit, and obey and conform
30 itself to the inner man and faith, and not rebel against them nor hinder
them, as is its nature to do if it is not kept under. For the inner man,
being conformed to God and created after the image of God through
faith, rejoices and delights itself in Christ, in whom such blessings have
been conferred on it, and hence has only this task before it: to serve God
35 with joy and for nought in free love. . . .

As Christ says, 'A good tree cannot bring forth evil fruit, neither can
a corrupt tree bring forth good fruit.' Now it is clear that the fruit does
not bear the tree, nor does the tree grow on the fruit; but, on the
contrary, the trees bear the fruit, and the fruit grows on the trees.

40 As then trees must exist before their fruit, and as the fruit does not
make the tree either good or bad, but, on the contrary, a tree of either
kind produces fruit of the same kind, so must first the person of the man
be good or bad before he can do either a good or a bad work; and his
works do not make him bad or good, but he himself makes his works
45 either bad or good. . . .

We do not then reject good works; nay, we embrace them and teach
them in the highest degree. It is not on their own account that we
condemn them, but on account of this impious addition to them and the
perverse notion of seeking justification by them. . . .

50 Lastly, we will speak also of those works which he performs towards
his neighbour. For man does not live for himself alone in this mortal
body, in order to work on its account, but also for all men on earth; nay,
he lives only for others, and not for himself. For it is to this end that he
brings his own body into subjection, that he may be able to serve others
55 more sincerely and more freely. . .Thus it is impossible that he should
take his ease in this life, and not work for the good of his neighbours,
since he must needs speak, act, and converse among men, just as Christ
was made in the likeness of men.

> Martin Luther, *Of the Liberty of a Christian Man*, 1520, in
> E. G. Rupp and B. Drewery, *Luther: Documents of Modern History*,
> 1970, pp. 50–3

Questions

a How is it possible for 'a Christian man' to be 'the most free lord of
all' and 'the most dutiful servant of all' (lines 2–3)?

b Why should Luther find it necessary to say that the effect of
Christian liberty 'is not that we should . . . lead a bad life' (line 10)?

c What distinction is Luther making between the scriptural
description of 'ministers, servants and stewards' (line 23) and
'Popes, bishops, and lords' (lines 22–3)?

d What, according to this passage, was the purpose of 'good works'
for 'the inner man' (line 30) and for 'his neighbour' (line 51)?

★　*e*　Why does Luther say that he 'embraces' 'good works' (line 46) but condemns the 'impious addition' (line 48) to them? In what way was this going against the teaching of the Roman Catholic church?

5   The Sacraments

I must deny that there are seven Sacraments, and must lay it down, for the time being, that there are only three, baptism, penance and the bread, and that by the court of Rome all these have been brought into miserable bondage, and the Church despoiled of all her liberty. . . .

5　　Formerly, when I was imbibing the scholastic theology, my lord the Cardinal of Cambray gave me occasion for reflection by arguing most acutely . . . that it would be much more probable, and that fewer superfluous miracles would have to be introduced, if real bread and real wine, and not only their accidents, were understood to be upon the
10　altar, unless the Church had determined the contrary. Afterwards, when I saw what the Church was which had thus determined . . . I became bolder; and whereas I had been before in great straits of doubt, I now at length established my conscience in the former opinion, namely, that there is real bread and real wine, in which is the real flesh and real blood
15　of Christ, in no other manner and in no less degree than the other party assert them to be under the accidents. . . .

　　I quite consent, then, that whoever chooses to hold either opinion should do so. My only object now is to remove scruples of conscience, so that no man may fear being guilty of heresy if he believes that real
20　bread and real wine are present on the altar. . . .

　　But why should not Christ be able to include His body within the substance of bread, as well as within the accidents? Fire and iron, two different substances, are so mingled in red-hot iron that every part of it is both fire and iron. Why may not the glorious body of Christ much
25　more be in every part of the substance of the bread? . . .

　　Concerning the Sacrament of Baptism . . . . This doctrine ought to have been studiously inculcated upon the people by preaching; this promise ought to have been perpetually reiterated; men ought to have been constantly reminded of their baptism; faith ought to have been
30　called forth and nourished. When this divine promise has been once conferred upon us, its truth continues even to the hour of our death; and thus our faith in it ought never to be relaxed, but ought to be nourished and strengthened, even till we die, by perpetual recollection of the promise made to us in baptism. . . .

35　Baptism then signifies two things: death and resurrection; that is, full and complete justification. When the minister dips the child into the water, this signifies death; when he draws him out again, this signifies life.

> Martin Luther, *On the Babylonish Captivity of the Church*, 1520, in
> E. G. Rupp and B. Drewery, *Luther: Documents of Modern History*,
> 1970, pp. 47–9

Questions

★ *a* What is a sacrament? Which sacraments of the Roman Catholic church is Luther 'denying' (line 1)?

   b What does Luther mean by 'fewer superfluous miracles would have to be introduced' (lines 7–8)?

   c What name is given to Luther's doctrine about communion? How does this passage help to explain what Luther meant by it?

   d Luther is not disagreeing with the traditional teaching of the church about baptism; what criticism of it is he making?

★ *e* In what ways did Luther's teaching about the sacraments change after the publication of the work from which this passage comes?

6 Problems concerning the Lord's Supper

(a) The Mass is an evil thing, and God is displeased with it . . . . It must be abolished. . . . I wish private masses abolished everywhere and only the ordinary evangelical Mass retained. Yet Christian love should not employ harshness here nor force the matter. However, it should be
5 preached and taught with tongue and pen that to hold mass in such a manner is sinful, yet no one should be dragged away from it by the hair. . . . We must first win the hearts of the people. . . In short, *I will preach it, teach it, write it, but I will constrain no man by force,* for faith must come freely without compulsion.

> Martin Luther, sermon on his return from exile, 1522, in S. E. Ozment, *The Reformation in the Cities*, 1975, p. 144

10 (b) I freely confess that if Carlstadt or any other could have convinced me five years ago that there was nothing in the sacrament but mere bread and wine, he would have done me a great service. I was sorely tempted on this point and wrestled with myself and tried to believe that it was so, for I saw that I could thereby give the hardest rap to the
15 papacy. I read treatises by two men who wrote more ably in defence of the theory than has Dr. Carlstadt and who did not so torture the Word to their own imaginations. But I am bound; I cannot believe as they do; the text is too powerful for me and will not let itself be wrenched from the plain sense by argument.
20 And if anyone could prove today that the sacrament were mere bread and wine, he would not much anger me if he was only reasonable. (Alas I am too much inclined that way myself when I feel the old Adam!) But Dr. Carlstadt's ranting only confirms me in the opposite opinion.

> Martin Luther to the Christians of Strasbourg, 14 December 1524, in P. Smith, *The Life and Letters of Martin Luther*, 1911, p. 239

(c) To the Evangelic Christians at Leipzig. Grace and peace in Christ,
25 who suffers and is put to death among you, but who will certainly rise and reign.

I have heard, dear friends, that some of you wish to know whether they may take the sacrament under one kind with good conscience, saying that if they only do that the government will be satisfied.
30 Although I know none of you nor how your hearts and minds are fixed, yet this is my counsel: Whosoever is convinced that God's Word commands the sacrament to be dispensed in both kinds should not do anything contrary to his conscience, for that would be tantamount to acting against God himself. And as Duke George [of Saxony] has
35 undertaken to search out the secrets of conscience, he will deserve to be deceived, as an apostle of the devil, which could easily be done, as he has no right to make such an inquiry, but sins against God and the Holy Ghost. And yet, as we must not do wrong because others do – though they be murderers and brigands – but must only decide what is right for
40 us to do, in the circumstances it would be better to say to the murderer and brigand openly: 'I will not do what you command; take my body and estate, and thereby injure him by whom you will be called to strict account, for Peter says "Jesus Christ is ready to judge the quick and the dead." Wherefore, dear brigand, go on as you like; what you will I will
45 not, but what I will, God will also, as you shall soon find out.' We must smite the devil in the face with the cross and not whistle to him nor flatter him, so that he will know with whom he has to do. May Christ our Lord strengthen you and be with you. Amen.

Martin Luther, 11 April 1533, in P. Smith *The Life and Letters of Martin Luther*, 1911, pp. 300–1

Questions

★ *a* What was the purpose of private masses?
★ *b* What had been happening in Wittenberg during Luther's absence to cause him to say 'I will constrain no man by force' (line 8)? How successful was Luther in dealing with the situation he found in Wittenberg?
   c In extract **(b)** why does Luther say he wishes Carlstadt had been able to change his belief? Why was Luther not persuaded?
   d Why did the 'Evangelic Christians at Leipzig' (line 24) want Luther's advice? What advice did he give them? In what sense was Duke George 'an apostle of the devil' (line 36)?

7 Introduction to the German Translation of the New Testament

Just as the Old Testament is a book in which are written God's laws and commandments, . . . so the New Testament is a book in which are written the gospel and the promises of God, together with the history of those who believe and of those who do not believe them. . . .
5   The gospel, then, is nothing but the preaching about Christ, Son of God and of David, true God and man, who by His death and resurrection has overcome for us the sin, death, and hell of all men who

believe in Him. Thus the gospel can be either a brief or a lengthy message; one person can write of it briefly, another at length. He writes
10 of it at length, who writes about many words and works of Christ, as do the four evangelists. He writes of it briefly, however, who does not tell of Christ's works, but indicates briefly how by His death and resurrection He has overcome sin, death, and hell for those who believe in Him, as do St. Peter and St. Paul.

15 See to it, therefore, that you do not make a Moses out of Christ, or a book of laws and doctrines out of the gospel, as has been done heretofore and as certain prefaces put it, even those of St. Jerome. For the gospel does not expressly demand works of our own by which we become righteous and are saved; indeed it condemns such works. Rather
20 the gospel demands faith in Christ: that He has overcome for us sin, death, and hell, and thus gives us righteousness, life, and salvation not through our works, but through His own works, death, and suffering, in order that we may avail ourselves of His death and victory as though we had done it ourselves. . . .

25 Hence it comes that to a believer no law is given by which he becomes righteous before God, as St. Paul says in I Timothy 1, because he is alive and righteous and saved by faith, and he needs nothing further except to prove his faith by works. Truly, if faith is there, he cannot hold back; he proves himself, breaks out into good works, confesses and
30 teaches this gospel before the people, and stakes his life on it. Everything that he lives and does is directed to his neighbor's profit, in order to help him – not only to the attainment of this grace, but also in body, property, and honor. Seeing that Christ has done this for him, he thus follows Christ's example. . . .

35 That is what Christ meant when at the last He gave no other commandment than love, by which men were to know who were His disciples and true believers. For where works and love do not break forth, there faith is not right, the gospel does not yet take hold, and Christ is not rightly known. See, then, that you so approach the books
40 of the New Testament as to learn to read them in this way.

Martin Luther, 1522, in H.J. Hillerbrand (ed.), *The Protestant Reformation*, 1968, pp. 38–42

Questions

a What is 'the gospel' (line 5)? Who were the 'four evangelists' (line 11) and Moses (line 15)?

★ b Who was St. Jerome (line 17) and what was his importance to Biblical scholarship?

c Why does a believer need to 'prove his faith by works' (line 29)? Why will he do this?

★ d What, according to Luther, is the purpose of reading 'the books of the New Testament' (lines 39–40)? How was the emphasis of Roman Catholic teaching different from that of Luther on this subject?

8 Understanding Scripture

I admit, of course, that there are many texts in the scriptures that are obscure and abstruse, not because of the majesty of their subject-matter, but because of our ignorance of their vocabulary and grammar; but these texts in no way hinder a knowledge of all the subject-matter of
5   scripture. . . .

The subject-matter of the scriptures, therefore, is all quite accessible, even though some texts are still obscure owing to our ignorance of their terms. Truly it is stupid and impious when we know that the subject-matter of scripture has all been placed in the clearest light, to call it
10   obscure on account of a few obscure words. If the words are obscure in one place, yet they are plain in another; and it is one and the same theme, published quite openly to the whole world, which in the scriptures is sometimes expressed in plain words, and sometimes lies as yet hidden in obscure words. . . .

15   To put it briefly, there are two kinds of clarity in scripture, just as there are also two kinds of obscurity: one external and pertaining to the ministry of the Word, the other located in the understanding of the heart. If you speak of the internal clarity, no man perceives one iota of what is in the scriptures unless he has the Spirit of God. All men have a
20   darkened heart so that even if they can recite everything in scripture, and know how to quote it, yet they apprehend and truly understand nothing of it. They neither believe in God, nor that they themselves are creatures of God. . . .

There is therefore another, an external judgement, whereby with the
25   greatest certainty we judge the spirits and dogmas of all men, not only for ourselves, but also for others and for their salvation. This judgement belongs to the public ministry of the Word and to the outward office, and is chiefly the concern of leaders and preachers of the Word. We make use of it when we seek to strengthen those who are weak in faith
30   and confute opponents. This is what we earlier called 'the external clarity of the holy scripture'. Thus we say that all spirits are to be tested in the presence of the Church at the bar of scripture. For it ought above all to be settled and established among Christians that the holy scriptures are a spiritual light far brighter than the sun itself, especially in things
35   that are necessary to salvation. But because we have for so long been persuaded of the opposite by the pestilential saying of the sophists that the scriptures are obscure and ambiguous, we are obliged to begin by proving even that first principle of ours by which everything else has to be proved – a procedure which among the philosophers would be
40   regarded as absurd and impossible.

Martin Luther, *De Servo Arbitrio*, 1525, in E. G. Rupp and B. Drewery (eds), *Luther: Documents of Modern History*, 1970, pp. 129–31

a   What criticism of scripture is Luther here replying to? What is the
     main line of his defence?
b   What does Luther argue is the only thing necessary for
     understanding scripture?
c   What is meant by 'dogmas' (line 25) and 'sophists' (line 36)?
d   The 'external judgement' (line 24) 'belongs to the public minstry of
     the Word' (line 27). Who is to make this judgement and for what
     purpose?
★ e   The work from which this extract is taken was written in reply to
     preaching by anabaptists. What particular points of their teaching
     are under attack here?

9   To the Christian Nobility of the German Nation

The Romanists have with great skill built three walls around
themselves, with which till now they have protected themselves so
that no one has been able to reform them; whereby all Christendom has
suffered woefully. In the first place, when attacked by the temporal
5   power they have laid it down that temporal power has no authority
over them, but that on the contrary the spiritual power is superior to the
temporal. Secondly, when Scripture was cited for their correction, they
have objected that no one may interpret Holy Writ except the pope.
Thirdly, when threatened with a General Council, they have invented
10 the notion that only the pope may call one. Thus privily robbing us of
three rods, they have escaped punishment; they have sat behind the safe
fortification of these three walls and practised all the villainy and
wickedness which now we see. . . .

Those now called spiritual – priests or bishops or pope – differ from
15 other Christians to no greater or more important degree than that they
shall administer the Word of God and the sacraments. That is their work
and office. The temporal power holds the sword and the rod to punish
evildoers and protect the pious. . . .

Now see in how Christian a manner they maintain and say that the
20 temporal arm is not superior to the spiritual and cannot control it. . . . Is
it not unnatural, let alone unchristian, for one member not to help
another and protect it against disaster? The more noble the member, the
more the rest ought to help it. Therefore I say, because the temporal arm
is ordained by God for the punishment of evildoers and protection of
25 the pious, its exercise is to be left free and unhindered throughout the
whole body of Christendom, not respecting any persons, be they pope,
bishop, parsons, monks, nuns, or whoever else. . . .

So I think the first paper wall is down. The temporal power has been
shown to be a member of the Body Christian and to be of the estate
30 spiritual, even though its occupation is in matters temporal. Therefore
its operation shall extend freely and without hindrance to all members

of the whole body; it shall punish and constrain where guilt merits it or need demands.

> Martin Luther, 1521, in G. R. Elton, *Renaissance and Reformation 1300–1648*, 1976, pp. 181–3

Questions

a   Who were 'the Romanists' (line 1)?

b   What is meant by 'the spiritual power is superior to the temporal' (lines 6–7)? Why does Luther disagree with this idea?

c   Why did Luther also disagree with the statement that 'no one may interpret Holy Writ except the pope' (line 8)?

★   d   Luther wrote the pamphlet from which this extract comes, in order to win support from the German nobles. What is there in its argument that was likely to appeal especially to these nobles? Why was Luther seeking the nobles' support for his cause?

10   Church Government

In the business of judging teaching and appointing and dismissing a teacher or pastor, one must pay absolutely no attention to any human law, regulation, tradition, usage, or custom, even if it is a law of pope or emperor, prince or bishop, or has been observed by half the world or all
5   of it, or has existed for one year or a thousand years. For the soul of man is an eternal thing, and above everything that is temporal. It must therefore be governed and shaped only by the eternal Word. For it is utterly ludicrous to govern the conscience of God with human laws and longstanding custom . . . . Christ establishes exactly the opposite: he
10   takes away from bishops, scholars, and councils both the right and the power to judge teaching, and he gives them to everyone and to all Christians in common. He says so in John 10: 'My sheep know my voice'. . . .

Here you see clearly who has the right to judge teaching, bishop,
15   pope, scholar – everyone has the right to teach; but the sheep should judge whether it is Christ's voice teaching or the voice of strangers. . . . Certainly there can be no false prophet amongst the hearers, but only amongst the teachers. Therefore all teachers should and must be subject to the judgement of the hearers, and so should their teaching. . . .
20   So now we conclude that where there is a Christian congregation which has the gospel, they not only have the right and power, but are obliged for their souls' salvation, according to the duty that they undertook to Christ in their baptism, to shun, flee from, set aside, and forsake the authority which the bishops, abbots, cloisters, seminaries,
25   and the like are now exercising, since it is quite obvious that they are teaching and ruling against God and his Word. . . .

But because a Christian congregation should not be without God's Word, and cannot be, it follows directly enough that it must have

teachers and preachers who promote that Word. Yet in this accursed last
30 time, the bishops and the false spiritual government are not and will not
be such teachers. They are also unwilling to provide or allow such
teachers. And as God is not to be asked to send a new preacher from
heaven, we must act according to Scripture, and from amongst
ourselves call and appoint those that are found fit for it, men whom God
35 has enlightened with understanding and has equipped with the necessary
gifts. For no one can deny that every individual Christian has God's
Word, is taught by God, and is his anointed priest. . . .

Moreover, even if our present bishops were men of integrity who
wanted to have the gospel and wanted to appoint preachers with
40 integrity, they could not and should not do even this without the
congregation's consent, choice, and calling, except where they are
forced by necessity so that souls will not be lost for want of God's
Word.

> Martin Luther, 1523, in I. D. K. Siggins (ed.), *Luther*, 1972,
> pp. 119–21

Questions

★ *a* Who are meant by the 'sheep' (line 15)? What do they, rather than
those in positions of authority, have a right to do? In what way had
Luther, in effect, recently put this idea into practice in Wittenberg?
 b What is meant by 'a Christian congregation which has the gospel'
(lines 20–1)? Why does this give them the duty to 'forsake the
authority' (line 24) of bishops and church institutions?
★ *c* What is this congregation to do about finding a preacher? On what
conditions does Luther say the bishops should appoint 'preachers
with integrity' (lines 39–40)? Why was this likely to offend the
Roman Catholic church?

11   Against the Heavenly Prophets

Herewith an answer has been given to several of Dr. Karlstadt's books.
We shall now give our attention to the book which has to do with the
Mass, so that we may deal specifically with the Sacrament. For I do not
know why he makes so many books, all of which deal with the same
5 subject. He could well put on one page what he wastes on ten. Perhaps
he likes to hear himself talk, as the stork its own clattering. For his
writing is neither clear nor intelligible, and one would just as soon make
one's way through brambles and bushes as read through his books. This
is a sign of the spirit. The Holy Spirit speaks well, clearly, in an orderly
10 and distinct fashion. Satan mumbles and chews words in his mouth and
makes a hundred into a thousand. It is an effort to ascertain what he
means. . . .

Observe carefully, my brother, this order, for everything depends on
it. However cleverly this factious spirit makes believe that he regards

15   highly the Word and Spirit of God and declaims passionately about love and zeal for the truth and righteousness of God, he nevertheless has as his purpose to reverse this order. His insolence leads him to set up a contrary order and, as we have said, seeks to subordinate God's outward order to an inner spiritual one. Casting this order to the wind with
20   ridicule and scorn, he wants to get to the Spirit first. Will a handful of water, he says, make me clean from sin? The Spirit, the Spirit, the Spirit, must do this inwardly. Can bread and wine profit me? Will breathing over the bread bring Christ in the sacrament? No, no, one must eat the flesh of Christ spiritually. The Wittenbergers are ignorant of this. They
25   make faith depend on the letter. Whoever does not know the devil might be misled by these many splendid words to think that five holy spirits were in the possession of Karlstadt and his followers.

    But should you ask how one gains access to this same lofty spirit they do not refer you to the outward gospel but to some imaginary realm,
30   saying: Remain in 'Self-abstraction' where I now am and you will have the same experience. A heavenly voice will come, and God himself will speak to you. If you inquire further as to the nature of this 'self-abstraction', you will find that they know as much about it as Dr Karlstadt knows of Greek and Hebrew. Do you not see here the devil,
35   the enemy of God's order? With all his mouthing of words, 'Spirit, Spirit, Spirit', he tears down the bridge, the path, the way, the ladder, and all the means by which the Spirit might come to you. Instead of the outward order of God in the material sign of baptism and the oral proclamation of the Word of God, he wants to teach you, not how the
40   Spirit comes to you but how you come to the Spirit. They would have you learn how to journey on the clouds and ride on the wind. They do not tell you how or when, whither or what, but you are to experience what they do.

    Martin Luther, 1525, in E. G. Rupp and B. Drewery, *Luther: Documents of Modern History*, 1970, pp. 118–19

Questions

★ *a* Who was Dr. Karlstadt? Why had he broken with Luther?

   b Why does Luther say, in the first paragraph, that Karlstadt's works are not the work of the Holy Spirit?

   c From this extract, what appears to have been Karlstadt's belief about 'the sacrament' (line 23)?

   d How does Luther substantiate his accusation that Karlstadt wishes 'to set up a contrary order' (lines 17–18)?

   e Why is Luther so critical of Karlstadt's 'mouthing of words' (line 35)?

IV   Other Reformers

Luther was so dominating a figure in the German Reformation that it is easy to ignore the other reformers, some of whom were remarkable men in their own right, who, at any other time, would no doubt have been much more widely known.

Philip Melanchthon (1497–1521) is probably the best-known today. An infant prodigy of learning, he was appointed the first professor of Greek at Wittenberg University at the age of twenty-one and his intellectual abilities were admired by both Erasmus and Luther. He quickly came under Luther's spell and was converted to his ideas. This was to be enormously important to the Reformation, as Melanchthon had a much clearer mind and style than Luther and it is to him that we owe the plainest expression of Lutheran theology, particularly the Augsburg Confession, the creed of the Lutheran Church.

Martin Bucer (1491–1551) has been described as the most influential reformer after Luther, Zwingli and Calvin. He began his career as a Dominican monk, but later was responsible for the introduction of the Reformation to Hesse and several German cities, most importantly Strasbourg, which became his base. He made several attempts to reconcile Luther and Zwingli and to reunite the reformers with the Roman Catholic Church, despite his own positive religious position. When Charles V imposed peace on the German Protestants in 1548, Bucer had to leave Strasbourg and came to England, where he spent the rest of his life. It was during his stay in England that he wrote his greatest work, *De Regno Christi*, which he dedicated to King Edward VI.

Of the other reformers represented in this chapter, Andrew Karlstadt (c.1480–1541) was one of Luther's first supporters but wanted to take reform much further than was generally acceptable and so had to leave Wittenberg. In later life he became more and more radical, trying to 'eradicate every non-Biblical element in the life of the Church' (A.G. Dickens).

Thomas Muntzer (c.1468–1525) also began as an admirer of Luther, but later denounced his teachings and became an advocate of social and religious revolution. Johann Eberlin von Gunzberg (c.1470–1533) was a Franciscan preacher converted to Luther's writings, who became an important Protestant pamphleteer, and Caspar Hedio (1494–1552) was a reformer who helped to consolidate the Protestant position in Strasbourg.

1   The Augsburg Confession

5. THE CHURCH'S MINISTRY. The Ministry of teaching the Gospel and offering the Sacraments is instituted that we may grasp this faith. For the Holy Spirit is given through the Word and the Sacraments, as it were through its instruments; and the Spirit creates
5   faith, where and when God sees fit, in those who hear the Gospel; and this is because God justifies – not through our merits but through Christ – those who believe that they are received through Christ into grace.

Our Churches condemn the Anabaptists and those who think that the Holy Spirit comes to men without an outward word, merely by their
10   own preparations and works. . . .

7. THE CHURCH. . . . For the Church is the congregation of the saints, in which the Gospel is rightly taught and the sacraments rightly administered. For the true unity of the Church it suffices to agree together concerning the teaching of the Gospel and the administration
15   of the Sacraments; it is not necessary that everywhere should exist similar traditions of men, or similar rites and ceremonies instituted by men.

8. THE NATURE OF THE CHURCH. Although the Church is, properly speaking, the congregation of the saints and true believers,
20   nevertheless, since many hypocrites and evildoers are mingled with them in this life, it is permissible to use the Sacraments which are administered by bad men. . .; and the Sacraments and the Word take their efficacy from the ordaining and the mandate of Christ, even if they are shown forth by bad men. . . .

25   9. BAPTISM. Baptism is necessary to salvation; through it is offered the grace of God; children should be baptized, so that, offered through baptism to God, they may be received into his grace.

10. THE LORD'S SUPPER. The body and blood of Christ are really present and are distributed in the Lord's Supper to those who eat; our
30   Churches reject those who teach otherwise.

22. Such are the main heads of our teaching, and in it nothing can be found differing from scripture, or from the Catholic Church, or from the Church of Rome as we understand it from its [classical] writers. We are not heretics. Our trouble is with certain abuses which have crept into
35   the Churches without any clear authority.

> Philip Melanchthon, 1530, in E. G. Rupp and B. Drewery, *Martin Luther: Documents of Modern History*, 1970, pp. 145–8

Questions

★   *a*   For what occasion did Melanchthon write the Augsburg Confession?

b   In what ways does this document show evidence of the reason for its compilation? What is there in it to explain why it was unacceptable to the Roman Catholic church?

c How does the first paragraph support Luther's belief in a form of predestination?

★ *d* What did Melanchthon (and Luther) mean about Christ being 'really present' in the Lord's Supper (line 28–9)? How did this differ from the teaching of the Roman Catholic Church?

e Explain how Melanchthon uses this document to dissociate his church from the Anabaptists.

2 Civil and Ecclesiastical Magistrates

This section on magistrates I consider very important. For the present I shall follow the popular division for pedagogical reasons. Some magistrates are civil and others ecclesiastical. The civil magistrate is one who bears the sword and watches over the civil peace. . . . Matters
5 under the sword are civil rights, civil ordinances of public courts, and penalties for criminals. It is the obligation of the sword to enforce the laws against murder, vengeance, etc. Therefore, the fact that the magistrate wields the sword is pleasing to God. . . . On wielding the power of the sword, I have this to say. In the first place, if rulers
10 command anything that is contrary to God, they must not be obeyed. . . .

In the next place, if they command anything that is for the public good, we must obey them in accordance with Romans 13:5: 'Therefore one must be subject, not only to avoid God's wrath, but also for the sake
15 of conscience.' For love constrains us to fulfill all civil obligations.

Finally, if anything is commanded with tyrannical caprice, we must bear with this magistracy also because of love, since nothing can be changed without a public uprising or sedition. Pertinent is Christ's word: 'But if anyone strikes you on the right cheek, turn to him the
20 other also.' . . .

As far as ecclesiastical magistrates are concerned, first, we think that bishops are servants and neither powers nor magistrates. Secondly, the bishops have no right to establish laws, since they have been enjoined to preach only the Word of God, not that of men. . . . Therefore, in the
25 first place, if they teach Scripture, they are to be heard as if Christ himself were speaking. . . .

Secondly, if they teach anything contrary to Scripture, they must not be listened to. . . . In these days the pope has decreed something contrary to divine justice in the bull by which Luther was condemned; in this he
30 must by no means be obeyed. . . .

In the fourth place, if you do not want to burden the conscience with the law of a bishop but interpret his command only as an external obligation (as spiritual men and those usually do who understand that the conscience can be bound by no human law), you will consider the
35 law of a bishop to be on a par with the tyranny of a civil magistrate. For whatever the bishops command that goes beyond Scripture is tyranny, since they do not have the right so to command.

Christ dispensed with the Pharisaic traditions . . . but he did not
uproot civil laws. Now that Pharisaic laws are dispensed with, we are
40 more free, not only because they are more a concern for each individual
than they are common burdens, but also because they easily ensnare the
conscience. The rule and direction of all human laws are under faith and
love, and especially under necessity. Necessity liberates from all
traditions if at any point either the soul or the life of the body has
45 fallen into danger through tradition.

> Philip Melanchthon, *Loci Communes*, 1521, in W. Pauck (ed.),
> *Melanchthon and Bucer: The Library of Christian Classics*, Vol. XIX,
> 1969, pp. 148–50

Question

a   What does Melanchthon mean by 'magistrates' (line l)?
b   Why is it 'pleasing to God' that 'the magistrate wields the sword'
    (line 8)?
★ c   Why was it particularly relevant in Germany to assert that bishops
    are 'neither powers nor magistrates' (line 22)? In what sense should
    they be regarded as 'servants' (line 22)?
d   Why did Melanchthon consider that bishops might act as tyrants?
    What were the implications of this for those who held the office of
    bishop?
e   What was the 'bull by which Luther was condemned' and why was
    it 'contrary to divine justice' (lines 28–9)?
f   In what ways did Melanchthon believe that Christians are now
    'more free' (line 40)?

3   Scripture and Justification

(a) I am discussing everything sparingly and briefly because the book is
to function more as an index than a commentary. I am therefore merely
stating a list of the topics to which a person roaming through Scripture
should be directed. Further, I am setting forth in only a few words the
5 elements on which the main points of Christian doctrine are based. I do
this not to call students away from the Scriptures to obscure and
complicated arguments but, rather, to summon them to the Scriptures if
I can.

For on the whole I do not look very favorably on commentaries, not
10 even those of the ancients. Far be it from me to call anyone away from
the study of canonical Scripture by too lengthy a composition of my
own! There is nothing I should desire more, if possible, than that all
Christians be occupied in greatest freedom with the divine Scriptures
alone and be thoroughly transformed into their nature. . . .
15 We have no other aim than to aid in every way possible the studies of
those who wish to be versed in the Scriptures. If my little book does not
seem to accomplish this, by all means let it perish, for it makes no
difference to me what people think about this publication. . . .

You have here, dear reader, as much concerning the power of innate
20 corruption as I thought ought to be said. Those who wish to be shaped
by the meditation and reading of Holy Writ rather than by human
commentaries will not require more. For no commentary can satisfy
those whose minds are confused by uncertain disputations and various
ideas and opinions of men; they understand nothing but the carnal. The
25 Holy Spirit is the one and only teacher, the most simple and the most
definite, who expresses himself most accurately and most simply in the
Holy Scriptures. When your mind has been transformed, as it were, into
these Scriptures, then you will comprehend absolutely, simply, and
exactly what is behind this fundamental point and other theological
30 matters as well. Those who depend not on the Spirit, but on the
judgment and opinion of men, do not see things as they are, but only
some vague shadows of things. . . .

(b) Why is it that justification is attributed to faith alone? I answer that
since we are justified by the mercy of God alone, and faith is clearly the
35 recognition of that mercy by whatever promise you apprehend it,
justification is attributed to faith alone. Let those who marvel that
justification is attributed to faith marvel also that justification is
attributed only to the mercy of God, and not rather to human merits.
For to trust in divine mercy is to have no confidence in any of our own
40 works. He who denies that the saints are justified by faith offends against
divine mercy. For since our justification is a work of divine mercy alone
and is not a merit of our own works, as Paul clearly teaches in Romans,
chapter 11, justification must be attributed to faith alone: faith is that
through which alone we receive the promised mercy.

> Philip Melanchthon, *Loci Communes* 1521, W. Pauck (ed.),
> *Melanchthon and Bucer: The Library of Christian Classics*, Vol.
> XIX, 1969, pp. 19–20, 46, 105

Questions

   a   Why does Melanchthon 'not look very favorably on commentaries'
       (line 9)?
★ *b*   What guide to understanding the Scriptures does he accept? In what
       way was this a new development in Christianity?
   c   What is meant by 'justification' (line 33)? How does Melanchthon
       believe that 'we are justified' (line 34)?
★ *d*   Explain in what ways this differed from the teachings of the Roman
       Catholic church and why it was so important to the early
       Lutherans.

4 The Kingdom of Christ and the Kingdoms of the World

The first point of similarity between the kingdoms of the world and the
Kingdom of Christ is that one person exercises the supreme power of

government. There is a difference, however, inasmuch as the kings of
the world, since they cannot be everywhere present with their subjects,
nor recognize and provide for their realms single-handedly, must
establish in various places, according to the size of their kingdoms,
representatives, vice-regents, and other authorities, and also have in their
power men outstanding in prudence and wisdom, whose counsel they
may use in their royal administration.

But our heavenly King, Jesus Christ, is, according to his promise,
with us everywhere and every day, 'to the consummation of the world'
(Matthew 28:20). He himself sees, attends to, and accomplishes whatever
pertains to the salvation of his own.

Therefore, he has no need of representatives to take his place. He does
use ministers, and certain specific kinds of offices for his work of
salvation, but their every work and labor is vain unless he himself gives
the growth to their planting and watering. . . . For they cannot even
think that they of themselves contribute to the administration of this
Kingdom whenever earthly kings have need of the kind of minister who
will help realize the royal decrees by using his own industry and
judgment, and perform the king's orders in a more effective way than
originally intended.

Secondly, the governance of the kingdoms of the world and of Christ
have this in common, that the kings of this world also ought to establish
and promote the means of making their citizens devout and righteous
who rightly acknowledge and worship their God and who are truly
helpful toward their neighbors in all their actions. . . .

Our heavenly King also attends to the details of providing and
making abundantly available the necessities of life to his subjects, so that
not a single one among his people shall be in need of these. For he
knows what things they need. . . . First of all, and this is also the duty of
the kings of the world, he sets each of his citizens, directly from
childhood, to encountering and learning the skills and functions for
which he himself has fashioned and fitted each individual. And he has so
distributed them that only in his Kingdom this end of civil government
is achieved. . . .

[The kings of the world] use external power and domain toward
these goals in such a way that not a single one of their subjects is in need,
but rather that enough will be available to each in order to live well and
happily. But they cannot give to those who abound in the blessings of
this life a willingness to share readily, or to those in need hearts that will
accept an unavoidable dependence on the kindness of others, whereas
our King, the dispenser of true love and patience, by his word and Spirit
renders the minds of his subjects as willing and strong as possible for this
salutary sharing of their wealth and patience in poverty.

Martin Bucer, *De Regno Christi*, 1550, in W. Pauck (ed.),
Melanchthon and Bucer: The Library of Christian Classics, Vol.
XIX, 1969, pp. 179–8

a   Why do kings need 'representatives, vice-regents and other authorities' (line 7)?

b   Why are ministers (of religion) necessary?

c   What does Bucer believe is 'the duty of the kings of the world' (lines 31–2)? Does he expect this to be achieved satisfactorily? What reasons does he give?

d   How far does the whole extract seem to you to be a practicable programme for a sixteenth century ruler?

★   e   Is there anything in this extract which could be cited as evidence that the work was written for the King of England and not for any German prince?

5   The Duties of a Christian Prince

When the ministers of the churches have been legitimately established and they rightly fulfill their office, all true kings and princes humbly hear the voice of Christ from the ministers and respect in them the majesty of the Son of God, as they administer not their own but only
5   the words and mysteries of Christ, the words and mysteries of eternal life.

But if our King, Christ, receives any people into his grace and favor, as of old he made the people of Israel a priestly kingdom, he sets over them princes and kings who, after the example of Moses and Joshua and
10   similar leaders and guardians of the people of God, are primarily concerned about instituting and promulgating religion and allow no one in the commonwealth to violate openly the covenant of the Lord, a covenant of faith and salvation, either by neglect of sacred ceremonies or fixed holidays, or by admitted wrongdoings and crimes, and still less by
15   contradiction or distortion of the Word of God.

It is the duty of all good princes to take every precaution to prevent any one of their subjects from doing injury to another, to prevent children from repudiating the guidance of their parents, slaves from escaping their masters or despising their commands, or anyone from
20   neglecting his duty to any other man. How much more, then, is it necessary to see to it that all governors of commonwealths, when they realise that all their power is from God alone and that he has appointed them shepherds of his people, govern and guard those subject to them according to his judgment, and take care lest any one of those entrusted
25   to them by God, their Maker, Father and Lord, should weaken in faith or abuse his laws or in any matter take away his honor from him. . . .

They shall take care, therefore, first of all, that the religion of Christ be administered by suitable priests of utmost sincerity and ardent zeal; next that according to the Lord's precept, whoever are consecrated to
30   Christ in Baptism be taught assiduously to observe whatever our King

has commanded. Nor shall anyone of their subjects contrive openly to subtract himself from the doctrine and discipline of Christ or have the impious audacity to be opposed to him. . . .

All the holy martyrs and Fathers have always recognized this, that it is
35 a supreme blessing of divine mercy for true kings and princes to be in charge of human affairs, that is, those who put the Kingdom of Christ first for themselves and take pains to spread it among their subjects day by day more fully. Therefore, the people of Christ, 'a royal priesthood, a holy nation, the special people of God' (I Peter 2:9–10), ought to rely
40 only on Christ its King and they should not be disturbed if the petty governments of the world are permitted to be in the hands even of savage tyrants. But they should pray continually to the Lord that he set true kings and princes over the commonwealths, who will administer all things according to his own heart. . . . And those whom God uses to
45 govern the nations ought, as I have said, to strive and labor for this above all, that they use their power according to the laws of God and according to the examples of pious princes commended by God.

> Martin Bucer, *De Regno Christi*, 1550, in W. Pauck (ed.), *Melanchthon and Bucer: The Library of Christian Classics*, Vol. XIX, 1969, pp. 188–91

Questions

★ *a* What does Bucer say is the source of the power of 'all governors of commonwealths' (line 21)? But what should their relationship be with ministers of the church? How does Bucer's opinion on this subject compare with Luther's?

   b Why is it a 'supreme blessing' (line 35) to be ruled by a prince?

★ *c* What is the first duty of a prince? What other duties follow from this? Why was this a particularly relevant point in a work dedicated to the King of England?

   d Why should 'the people of Christ . . . not be disturbed' if they are ruled even by 'savage tyrants' (lines 38–42)? In the light of this extract, what do you think Bucer would regard as 'tyrannical' rule?

6 The Christian Life

The Kingdom of our Savior Jesus Christ is that administration and care of the eternal life of God's elect, by which this very Lord and King of Heaven by his doctrine and discipline, administered by suitable ministers chosen for this very purpose, gathers to himself his elect, those dispersed
5 throughout the world who are his but whom he nonetheless wills to be subject to the powers of the world. He incorporates them into himself and his Church and so governs them in it that purged more fully day by day from sins, they live well and happily both here and in the time to come. . . .

10   It is a principal function of kings and of governors to search and explore what function of life has been designed by God for each citizen, and to take care that each one is initiated, prepared, and helped toward this end from childhood, so certainly the same persons ought to exercise utmost interest and a primary concern among their subjects, and,
15 wherever possible, to seek and find those whom the Lord seems to have appointed to this supremely salutary work, necessary before all others, of preaching the gospel. . . . They should take care that such of these as they can discover be initiated and trained from childhood for this most holy office, and that those who have been duly tested and proved be
20 used in their good time for this function. . . .

Nor is it sufficient for the kindness of Christians to give food, shelter, and clothing to those in extreme need; they should give so liberally of the gifts of God which they have received that they may even be able . . . to endow and help marriageable girls who are honest and
25 devout, who, because they are without dowry, are kept from marriage longer than is fair, so that they can be married in due time and joined to suitable husbands; they should help boys of outstanding ability who have no patrons to be educated toward studying for the sacred ministry of the Church; finally, they should help, both by gifts and loans, faithful
30 men who are unemployed, that they can make a living by their trade and feed their children and educate them in the Lord and show themselves more profitable citizens of the commonwealth.

      Martin Bucer, *De Regno Christi*, 1550, W. Pauck (ed.), *Melanchthon and Bucer: The Library of Christian Classics*, Vol. XIX, 1969, pp. 225, 227, 315

Questions

a   What is meant by 'God's elect' (line 2) and the 'commonwealth' (line 32)?

b   Why would many people in the twentieth century disagree with Bucer's argument in the second paragraph?

★   c   How far has 'the kindness of Christians' (line 21) been replaced by government action today? Is this preferable?

d   What does Bucer regard as the only important career for boys? Why did he think this?

7 The Priesthood of All Believers

All Christians are parsons, for they are built upon the one stone who makes them parsons. . . . So are they a spiritual house, a holy priesthood, to offer spiritual sacrifices . . . . From which it follows that faith in Christ makes all believers into priests or parsons, and that the parsons receive
5 nothing new when they are consecrated, but are only chosen to the office and service. . . .

In this matter I know neither father nor mother, but I follow divine Scripture alone which cannot err or deceive me, even though at the same time I suffer shame, derision, poverty, misery. . . . I know I must
10 be resigned and that I must resign all creatures. I know that I cannot be a disciple and follower of Christ, unless I renounce father and mother, brother and sister and friends, my own nature, skin and hair – all must be renounced, all within and all without me, for I know there is no higher virtue in heaven and earth than resignation. . . .
15 It is always less dangerous to stay in than go out – it is dangerous indeed to deal inwardly with the word of God, when the soul hears it freshly from God – it is much more dangerous to break out with it and press with it through the ranks of one's enemies. None the less I must let God's will be done and the unsurrenderedness and love of my own soul
20 will become the reproach of mine enemies, and a fiery purgatory. For we must all be conformed to Christ and follow in his steps, and so I ought to preach Christ not in a corner but in the midst of the congregation. . . .
    God's commandment stands to all fathers, that they should teach their
25 children and servants. Every man is bound to preach God's Word in house or at table, morning or evening, in field or barn, whether at leisure or at work, and he is to study God's Word and treat of it to those who are round him, or who belong to him. This is a universal command addressed to all who understand God's Word and God has made them
30 all through this commandment to be priests, all men to whom he has universally revealed it. For nobody is excluded, because God's commands pertain to all men, and touch the love and honour of God and his neighbour.

Andrew Karlstadt, 1520, in Gordon Rupp, *Patterns of Reformation*, 1969, pp. 84–5, 123

Questions

a What does Karlstadt mean by saying that 'all Christians are parsons' (line l)?
b In what ways should 'all fathers' (line 24) carry out what would normally be regarded as the duties of a parson? What, then, does Karlstadt say is the purpose of consecrating some men to be 'parsons'?
c Why does he say 'I must be resigned' (lines 9–10)?
★ d What practical consequences for the church resulted from the development of this doctrine of the priesthood of all believers?

8 (a) Criticism of the Clergy

Our clergy make heavy the light law of Christ against his command. They entangle our consciences in hellish scruples by subjecting us to so many papal laws and human traditions, so many censures under threat of the ban, irregularity, or interdict, and so many ordinances on fasting, celebrating, eating, drinking – from all of which Christ has set us free. They lay on us so many contrived and foolish rules for confessing, when the Christian church asks of us only a sincere and trusting acknowledgement of our sin to the priest without any special anxious enumeration. They subject us to manifold penances which God has not commanded. . . . They burden us with the great deception of indulgence – letters of indulgence and the reservation and dispensation of so many types and cases of conscience – and the theft of our benefices and endowed preachers by honorless, soulless, deceitful, fat and lazy people known as courtiers, who come and go daily. These are the things that daily vex the consciences and plague the possessions of German people.

(b) Wolfaria, an ideal Protestant Land

Local government shall have power over the clergy as over all other people and shall not be hindered in judging and punishing priests who betray their trust as they judge and punish other public criminals. . . .

Monasteries shall be nothing more than schools for the young, where boys and girls are taught Christian commandments and discipline. . . .

It is desired that all will seek at least once each year the counsel or special instruction of their priest or chaplain. An instruction to do so shall be publicly proclaimed once each year in the marketplace, although no one is obliged to confess his secrets to the priest unless he wishes to do so. . . .

Mass is to be read only on holidays and in the presence of the assembled community and with common prayer. . . .

Bread and wine are to be given to all in the Eucharist and, save for public sinners, without prevenient confession. Five sacraments are to be observed: baptism, Eucharist, absolution, prayer and 'diligent observance of God's word'. Children are to be baptised as infants. . . .

All prayers save the Lord's Prayer are forbidden as a capital offense. Only common Christian doctrines are permitted, and only the Apostle's Creed may be sung in church.

Johann Eberlin von Gunzberg, c.1521, in S. E. Ozment, *The Reformation in the Cities*, 1975, pp. 96–7, 99–102

Questions

a   What is meant by 'they entangle our consciences in hellish scruples' (line 2) and 'benefices' (line 12)?

b   In what ways could an indulgence be described as a 'great deception' (line 10)?

★ c   Why would many people have agreed with Eberlin that these things particularly 'vex' and 'plague' the 'German people' (line 15)?

d What criticisms of the Roman Catholic church are implicit in the
description of Wolfaria?

★ *e* In what ways is Wolfaria a less radically reformed state than would
have been advocated by Luther?

9 Magistrate's Sermon, Strasbourg, 1534

(a) Many have thrown off the papacy and slipped out from under its
heavy human yoke. But they do not now want to take up the gospel
and place themselves under the light yoke of Christ. Many no longer go
to papist confession, but they also do not go to Christian confession.

5   One no longer prays, fasts, or gives alms as was done under the papacy.
But one also does not do as one should in a true Christendom. One no
longer hears mass, but then one also does not hear the gospel. Before
there were many holidays, but now one doesn't even observe Sunday.
With what terrible laziness the priests, monks, and nuns used to devour

10   the income and goods of the church. All they did was eat, drink, and
frolic about in the most offensive ways. But now it is the workers and
the youth who run wild, and many have no respect for God, worship,
good works, or any honorable thing. The same is true for the peasantry
on the land.

15   (b) We read of Pericles the Athenian that when he went into the council
chamber and put on his robes he thought all the time about those over
whom he ruled, remembering that they were Athenian citizens, free and
Greek. So should you [the Strasbourg magistracy] now ponder that
those over whom you rule are citizens of Strasbourg, which shall be a

20   city of God. Remember that they too are free men, for Christ has freed
them from their sins, and they should live a new life as citizens of
heaven. Remove false teaching from their midst, guide them with true
doctrine and every good order and policing. Care for them, work for
them, turn to them your every energy, for it is to you and to them a

25   matter of eternal life.

> Caspar Hedio, in Steven E. Ozment, *The Reformation in the Cities*,
> 1975, p. 154, 212–13

Questions

a What does the author mean by 'one also does not hear the gospel'
(line 7)?

b What criticism is he making of the papacy?

★ *c* What reason does the author give for so many people having 'no
respect for God, worship or good works' (lines 12–13)? Can you
find any evidence elsewhere which supports or conflicts with this
evidence?

d   Do you think that extract **(b)** would really have encouraged the magistrates to make Strasbourg 'a city of God' (line 20)?

10   The Gospel according to Thomas Muntzer

The Elect man will find that all the Fathers, Patriarchs, the prophets, and especially the apostles, have come to faith only through great difficulty, not like those crack-brained easygoing swine at Wittenberg who are scared by the hurricane of roaring waters and the great floods of
5   wisdom. . . .

If a man had neither seen nor heard the Bible all his life, yet through the teaching of the Spirit he would have an undeceivable Christian faith, like all those who without books wrote the Holy Scripture. Even if you had swallowed the Bible whole, it is of no avail, you must suffer the
10   sharp ploughshare, or you have no faith. . . .

What a man hears or sees, that which shows him Christ, he receives as a wonderful Witness through which to hunt down, kill and crush his unbelief. So much so that he sees the whole of Holy Scripture as a two-edged Sword, for all that is contained in it is to this end, that it should
15   always kill us rather than make us live. . . .

[A Covenanted Band] is only intended as a threat to the godless, that they should restrain their violence until the Elect stand up to them with their exploration of God's Art and Wisdom as Witness. When the godly make a covenanted association, although there are bad people within,
20   they will not accomplish their will, for the loyal freedom of the good will give them less room to do ill than otherwise, so that the whole company may not be blamed. The Covenanted Band is nothing but an Emergency Device which is to be denied to no one, according to the natural judgement of all rational men. . . .

25   I preach such a Christian faith as does not agree with that of Luther, but which is in conformity with the hearts of the elect in all the world. And even though he were born a Turk, a man might yet have the Beginning of this same faith, that is, the moving of the Holy Ghost. . . .

If I am to be given a hearing before Christendom, then those ought to
30   be informed, bidden, invited from all nations of men who have suffered invincible temptation, found despair in their hearts and through the same been all the time brought to remembrance. Those are the people I will admit to be my judges.

> Thomas Muntzer, in Gordon Rupp, *Patterns of Reformation*, 1969, pp. 260, 273–4, 299–300, 328–9

Questions

a   Who or what were by 'the Fathers' (line 1), the 'swine at Wittenberg' (line 3), the 'Elect' (line 17), and 'a Covenanted Band' (line 22)?

b Why does Muntzer regard 'Holy Scripture as a two-edged Sword' (lines 13–14)

c In what ways was Muntzer preaching 'a Christian faith as does not agree with that of Luther' (line 25)?

V Anabaptism

Anabaptism means re-baptism and is used to describe those who did not believe in infant baptism, but only in the use of baptism as a kind of confirmation for people who were already believers. It can be said to have begun in 1525 'when a former priest in the home of a university-educated prophet of the new order received baptism on confession of sin from the hand of a layman' (G. H. Williams).

Beyond that it is difficult to define anabaptism. It was never an organised church but a number of sects which formed and re-formed in different parts of Europe, having little in common except their practice of adult baptism. There were inevitable divisions between them, and between them and Catholics and Lutherans, about the practice and interpretation of communion, the doctrine of the Trinity and other matters, because the Anabaptists believed that every individual had the right to interpret Scripture for him or herself and so a great many different interpretations were propounded.

The events at Munster marked a tragic climax in the development of Anabaptism, but the movement was too diverse to be destroyed by this disaster. It survived in Europe, and later in North America, despite severe persecution, partly because it was not an organised movement, so that an attack on one area or group did not affect others, who anyway expected persecution.

This persecution was not only the result of their religious beliefs but also their political attitude. Rejection of infant baptism meant rejection of the church at a time when church membership was part of membership of the state and so could give rise to accusations of treason. The Anabaptists also believed in the separation of church and state. This led to a refusal to take their share in local government, to pacifism and to a rejection of the need to swear oaths, all of which made them unacceptable to government authorities. It must be said that they usually accepted the inevitable punishment meekly but many were put to death for their beliefs. Even so the movement was never wholly destroyed, though it was largely driven underground or to other parts of Europe than Germany.

1 An Appeal to the Bohemian Nation

I, Thomas Muntzer of Stolberg, confess before the whole Church and the whole world, wherever this letter may be displayed, that I can bear witness, with Christ and all the Elect who have known me from my

youth up, that I have used my utmost diligence, above all other men,
that I might have or attain a higher understanding of holy invincible
Christian faith. . . . I have not learned from any Scholar the true Order
of God which he has set in all creatures, not the least word, and that the
Whole pefect work is the way to understand the Parts – these are never
to be obtained from those who set up to be true Christians, especially
from those damned parsons. It is true I have heard from them about the
bare word of Scripture, which they have stolen, like thieves and
murderers from the Bible. . . .

Now the world (led astray through many sects) has long desired
exceedingly to know the truth, so that the saying of Jeremiah has come
true: the children have asked for bread, but there was nobody to break it
to them. . . . They have not explained the true Spirit of the Fear of the
Lord which would have taught them they are irrevocably God's
children.

So it comes about that Christians (to defend the truth) are about as
competent as knaves, and dare in consequence to jabber in lordly fashion
that God does not speak with men any longer, just as though he had
now become dumb. And they think it is enough that it would be
written down in their books. . . .

When the New Church begins, this nation shall be a mirror to the
whole world. Therefore I appeal to Everyman, to come to the defence
of God's Word. . . . If you will not do this, then God will let you be
beaten by the Turk in the coming Year. I know truly what I am saying,
that it is so. Therefore I will suffer those things which Jeremiah had to
suffer. Take this to heart, dear Bohemians, I demand an account of you,
not only such as Peter teaches but as God himself demands. I will give
account to you also, and, if I do not in fact possess the knowledge of
which I boast so openly, then am I a child of temporal and eternal death.
I can give no higher pledge. Christ be with you.

Given at Prague in 1521 on All Saints' Day.

Thomas Muntzer, in Gordon Rupp, *Patterns of Reformation*, 1969,
pp. 175–8

Questions

a Why did Muntzer think that parsons were 'like thieves and
   murderers' (lines 11–12) in their use of the Bible?
b What are 'sects' (line 13)? How have they 'led astray' 'the world'
   (line 13)?
c In what way would Muntzer's 'New Church' be 'a mirror to the
   whole world' (lines 24–5)?
★ d Why might Muntzer think that the Bohemians would be more
   receptive than others to his teachings?

2 Extracts from the Writings of Caspar Schwenckfeld

(a) We are prone to swerve from the left hand to the right, contrary to the Lord's command. Turn not to the right nor to the left. We must walk on the royal road and seek to find the medium between the former hypocritical life and the present liberty. Otherwise all will be futile.

An Admonition to All the Brethren in Silesia, 11 June 1524.

5 (b) Although it is impossible for the old corrupt man to keep the commandments of God, as loving God with thy whole heart and thy neighbor as thyself, which is the fulfilling of the law, it is not impossible for the new regenerated man, that is, for all Christians who believe in Christ, to keep them.

10 (c) In the morning as I awoke for the day and softly the [thought of the] eucharist returned to my heart, and behold after an interval there surged within me a tremendous force (as when a light suddenly appears in the darkness) which completely absorbed me and endowed with much wisdom led me to the understanding of the eucharist; for it went
15 through the whole of my body but especially my head and opened up to me, as in the twinkling of the eye, all texts bearing upon the eucharist and the action at the Last Supper, speaking to me with a corporeal voice. . . and showed the proper order of the words of the Supper. . . . That neither Luther has taught correctly about the sacrament nor
20 Zwingli hit upon the right way in respect to the action of the sacrament of thanksgiving [is clear], for the words of the Dominical Supper must be weighed and compared with John 6:55: My flesh *est* flesh indeed; and that the words This *est* my body are the same as: My flesh *est* food indeed [now and forever more].

25 (d) We . . . confess and find ourselves in duty bound, and wholly trust no one will find reason to criticize this our Christian and just purpose, or to think ill of the fact that we admonish men in this critical time to suspend for a time the observance of the highly venerable sacrament, and first to concern themselves through the Word of God about the
30 thing most needful . . . in order that we and other ministers of the Word will not be casting that which is holy unto the dogs.

Caspar Schwenckfeld, in G. H. Williams, *The Radical Reformation*, 1962, pp. 107, 110, 111–12, 114

Questions

a   Schwenckfeld sought a middle way between Roman Catholicism and Lutheranism. How does he characterise these in extract (a)?

b   Why did Schwenckfeld feel that he was correct in his belief about the eucharist and Luther and Zwingli were not?

c How did Schwenckfeld propose, in extract **(d)**, to overcome the problems caused by the variety of interpretations of the eucharist being propounded in the 1520s?

d What kind of a Christian life is Schwenckfeld expecting of those who agree with him?

3 The Schleitheim Confession of Faith, 1527

Dear brethren and sisters, we who have been assembled in the Lord at Schleitheim . . . make known in points and articles to all who love God that as concerns us we are of one mind to abide in the Lord as God's obedient children, His sons and daughters, we who have been and shall
5 be separated from the world in everything, and completely at peace. . . .

Baptism shall be given to all those who have learned repentance and amendment of life, and who believe truly that their sins are taken away by Christ, . . . and to all those who with this significance request baptism of us and demand it for themselves. This excludes all infant baptism, the
10 highest and chief abomination of the pope.

All those who wish to break one bread in remembrance of the broken body of Christ, and all who wish to drink of one drink as a remembrance of the shed blood of Christ, shall be united beforehand by baptism in one body of Christ which is the church of God and whose
15 Head is Christ. . .

A separation shall be made from the evil and from the wickedness which the devil planted in the world; in this manner, simply that we shall not have fellowship with them, the wicked, and not run with them in the multitude of their abominations. . . . From all this we should learn
20 that everything which is not united with our God and Christ cannot be other than an abomination which we should shun and flee from. By this is meant all popish and anti-popish works and church services, meetings and church attendance, drinking houses, civic affairs, the commitments made in unbelief and other things of that kind, which are highly
25 regarded by the world and yet are carried on in flat contradiction to the command of God, in accordance with all the unrighteousness which is in the world. . . .

The sword is ordained of God outside the perfection of Christ. It punishes and puts to death the wicked, and guards and protects the
30 good. In the perfection of Christ, however, only the ban is used for a warning and for the excommunication of the one who has sinned, without putting the flesh to death. . . . Finally it will be observed that it is not appropriate for a Christian to serve as a magistrate . . . the government magistracy is according to the flesh, but the Christians' is
35 according to the Spirit . . . The worldlings are armed with steel and iron, but the Christians are armed with the armour of God.

H. J. Hillerbrand (ed.), *The Protestant Reformation*, 1968, pp. 129–34

a   Why did this Confession exclude 'all infant baptism' (line 9)?

b   In the list of things which 'we should shun and flee from' (line 21), which caused the greatest problems for secular authorities in dealing with these people, and why?

c   What is meant by 'the ban' (line 30)?

d   Why is it 'not appropriate for a Christian to serve as a magistrate' (line 33)?

4   An Anabaptist Defends His Beliefs

Then [Sattler] spoke and answered without fear. To the first [accusation]: that we have acted against the imperial command we do not admit; for that says that one should not adhere to Luther's doctrine and delusion but only to the gospel and the Word of God; and so have we done. For I
5   do not know that I have acted contrary to the gospel or the Word of God; let this be proved by the word of Christ.

To the second: that the sacrament does not contain the real body of our Lord Jesus Christ, that we admit; for the Scripture says thus: Christ ascended into heaven and sits on the right hand of his heavenly father
10   where he will judge the quick and the dead. It follows that if he be in heaven and not in the bread, he cannot be eaten corporeally.

To the third: concerning baptism we say: infant baptism is not useful for salvation, for it is written that we live by faith alone. Also he who believes and is baptised shall be saved. . . .
15   To the fifth: . . . Concerning the saints, we say that we who live and believe are the saints. . . .

To the sixth: we hold that we are not to take an oath to the authorities, for the Lord says (Matt. 5.34–7) 'Swear not at all . . . but let your communication be Yea, Yea, Nay, Nay.' . . .
20   To the eighth: if the Turk comes he shall not be resisted, for it is written, Thou shalt not kill. We are not to defend ourselves against the Turk and other persecutors, but are to pray heartily to God that He be our protection and defence. That I said that if war were right I would rather fight against the supposed Christians who persecute, hunt and kill
25   true Christians than against the Turk, was for this reason. The Turk is a true Turk and knows nothing of the Christian faith; he is a Turk in the flesh. So you would be Christians and boast of Christ, but persecute Christ's true witnesses and are Turks in the spirit.

> Michael Sattler, in G. R. Elton, *Renaissance and Reformation 1300–1648*, 1976, pp. 197–8

Questions

a   Explain Sattler's defence to the first accusation.

b   Why was infant baptism 'not useful for salvation' (lines 12–13)?

★   *c*   What did the Anabaptists mean by 'the saints' (line 15)?

d In his defence against the eighth accusation (lines 20–8), why does Sattler refuse to fight against the Turk and why would his defence be totally unacceptable to those accusing him?

★ *e* Sattler was one of those who drew up the Schleitheim Confession (extract 3 above). How far do the accusations here suggest that he had been trying to follow the way of life embodied in the Confession?

5 The Trial of Augustin Würzlburger, 1528

Hans Sedlmair, of Oberhaim, confesses and states that one Augustin Würzlburger, of Regensburg, had visited him last Lent; he could not recall the exact date. This Augustin had talked about the gospel and asserted that to eat meat during Lent was not sinful. Also, our first
5   baptism was invalid, for God Himself had said: 'He who believes and is baptized, shall be saved; he who does not believe, shall be condemned.' . . .

Hans Sedlmair further confesses and states that Augustin visited him again on April 14, [1528], at his house at Oberhaim and from a book
10   proclaimed to him and Hans Weber, who was also arrested, the gospel. Augustin asked him if he believed in our Lord Jesus Christ who suffered death and pain on the cross. He answered affirmatively and Würzlburger inquired of him if he desired from the bottom of his heart to be baptized? He had answered affirmatively. Afterwards
15   Augustin brought water into the stable in a small pitcher, took some water with his hands and baptized him in the name of the Father, Son, and Holy Spirit. . . After Würzlburger had baptized him, he prohibited him to attend church, unless the gospel was preached. If he went to church, he should not remove his hat. . . .
20   Augustin Würzlburger was interrogated . . . . There were many apostles among them and wherever one is sent, he has to go and preach, even if it should cause death. They did not mean to offend anyone. There was no special directive concerning food; he had eaten meat during Lent when it was available. . . . He said that all this he clearly
25   found in Scripture. If he were taught better and differently, he would desist. . . .

He had preached to them the gospel of all creatures, that they might recognize God and also how they were to live, and he had also told them that if they follow Christ they would be persecuted. If they
30   wanted to accept this, they should do it. Thereupon they did accept it and surrendered to the discipline of the Father and the pure word of God to live henceforth according to the commands of God. . . .

On Saturday, October 10, Augustin N., a teacher and Anabaptist, was led to the city hall, placed on a bench, where he was charged with
35   having been rebaptized and himself afterwards rebaptizing others, nine persons all in all. . . . Even though he had deserved, according to

imperial law, death by burning, the Council had mercifully ruled that he was to be executed by beheading.

Edited by H. J. Hillerbrand (ed.), *The Protestant Reformation*, 1968, pp. 137–142

Questions

a   What was meant by the prohibition to attend church 'unless the gospel was preached' (line 18)?
b   What did Würzlburger mean by 'apostles' (line 21)?
c   In what ways does this extract support the contention that 'if they follow Christ they would be persecuted' (line 29)?
★ d   Why did these confessions make Sedlmair and his friends unacceptable to both Roman Catholics and Lutherans?

6   Some Anabaptist Teachings

(a) And now in this final age the true apostolic emissaries of the Lord Jesus Christ will gather the elect flock and call it through the gospel and lead the Bride of the Lord into the spiritual wilderness, betroth, and covenant her through baptism to the Lord. . . .

5   When . . . the bride of the Lord Jesus Christ has given herself over to the Bridegroom in baptism, which is the sign of the covenant, and has betrothed herself and yielded herself to him of her own free will . . . thereupon the Bridegroom and exalted Lord Jesus Christ comes and by his hand – the apostolic emissaries are the hand – takes bread (just as a
10   bridegroom takes a ring or a piece of gold) and gives himself to his bride with the bread . . . and takes also the chalice with the wine and gives to his bride with the same his true bodily blood . . . in such as way that the Bridegroom and the outpouring of his blood is [one] with hers. . . . She [is] in him and, again, he is in her, and they together are thus one body,
15   one flesh, one spirit, and one passion, as bridegroom and bride!

Melchior Hofmann, *The Ordinance of God*, 1530, in G. H. Williams, *The Radical Reformation*, 1962, p. 308

(b) These things can be understood by no one fully in the first adolescence, because at this stage that spirit of divinity is submerged in the storms of youth and that hidden fire [the Spirit] is unable to be felt amidst the flowing saps of maturing flesh. Just as an adolescent is not
20   really fitted to grasp ethical teachings, so also he is not fitted to understand the gospel, however much he may be instructed at this time. Therefore Christ after the earlier period of instruction set forth as the proper age for baptism that of thirty years. . . .

Serpentine knowledge, when we begin to taste it, drives us into sin
25   and hurls us into a kind of abyss of death, so that a new kind of death requires a new kind of life through Christ, a spiritual death, a spiritual life. There follows here by a certain antithesis a true measure of

penitence, faith, and baptism. . . . In this mystery, our sins having been
forgiven, Christ again, through the Holy Spirit, endows us with the
30   knowledge of good and evil and deifies us with a new deity, freeing us
from the serpentine deity, which is the wisdom of the world. . . .

Baptism is, having heard the word of the gospel, in the unity of faith,
to be cleansed by the laver of water into the unity and fellowship of the
spotless heavenly Church. In infant baptism no spiritual church is
35   assembled, but a Babylonian chaos.

> Michael Servetus, *Restitutio Christianismi*, 1533, in G. H. Williams,
> *The Radical Reformation*, 1962, pp. 313–16

(c) I say therefore, that if thou art a believer in Christ and art mindful in
thine heart of Almighty God, that he is thy gracious Father . . and art
mindful of Jesus Christ's becoming man and of his bitter suffering . . .
and believest that all such has happened for thine own good unto the
40   resurrection and eternal life. . . whenever that takes place in the heart of
anybody, regardless of where that person is – hewing timber or cleaning
a stall, washing dishes or sweeping the house, ploughing the field or
mowing the meadow, yea, tending the cattle in the pasture – when such
thoughts are opened up within, that person with certainty tastes the
45   body and the blood of Christ, and he does so although there be no
priest, no altar, and no outward sign.

> Clement Ziegler, 1524, in G. H. Williams, *The Radical
> Reformation*, 1962, p. 337–8

Questions

a   What is meant by 'the true apostolic emissaries' (line 1) and 'the
elect flock' (line 2)?
b   Hofmann envisages either individuals or all the elect as 'the Bride of
the Lord' (line 3). How do his ideas about communion compare
with those of Ziegler in extract **(c)**?
c   Why was adolescence not regarded as an appropriate time for
baptism?
★   d   Why does Ziegler say that 'no priest, no altar and no outward sign'
(lines 45–6) are necessary for communion with Christ? Why would
this have been unacceptable to all Christians who were not
Anabaptists?

7   Events at Munster

(a) A Letter to the Duke of Cleves, March 1534

Your grace, be assured of our willing and faithful service at all times.

Some of those from Munster, who call themselves prophets or
preachers . . . have been in [your] lands . . . and were asked by some
subjects of your grace that they should go to Munster with them and
5   there see the wonderful signs and works and listen to the prophets.

And so about forty of them . . . went by boat to Dusseldorf. And we have now found that these same forty have arrived here in Dusseldorf and have been arrested.

Among them is one called Jacob van Osnabruck who confesses that
10 he was sent into the lands of your grace to tell the common, simple people about the signs and wonders which have happened in Munster; and . . . he had shown the common, simple man such things that some of them have left their own and followed him.

(b) From the confessions of Jacob van Osnabruck

At Easter [1533] he went from Osnabruck to Munster and there he was
15 an apprentice with a master. . . .

In Munster he has seen wonderful things in heaven and on earth, especially with the uproar that took place where father and son, mother and daughter separated from each other and each according to their own reasoning went in different directions. Also, Knipperdollinck, who is of
20 the right spirit, had heard wonderful things from heaven and he called out: better yourselves, better yourselves, the Lord is coming; and also his wife . . . called out from the spirit: better yourselves, better yourselves, then the king of Zion will come and rebuild Jerusalem; and many more who also had the spirit have called out the same and called for penitence.

25 There is supposed to be a prophet from Leyden whose name he does not know [Johann Matthys from Harlem] who has been sent like Enoch and another one, a prophet . . . called Melchior Hoffman, who has been sent like Helias as messenger for the great day of the Lord.

So he, Jacob, has confessed that [he] has told the people that the world
30 is going to be cruelly punished between now and Easter, that less than a tenth of the people will survive; only in Munster there will be peace and safety, because it is the city of the Lord and the new Jerusalem, where the Lord will save his people and everyone will have enough to live on.

He also confessed that he told the people, that the Christians in
35 Munster should give their houses and beds to all Christians who arrive and help them and give them food and drink, money and clothes. Then the preachers said that the city will be so full of people that houses should be built for the Christians in the yard of the cathedral, in the cathedral and churches and so at last the people shall gather and should
40 be looked after with the help of the houses and goods of the heathens and godless. . . .

Generally it is said in Munster that all dealings by the clergy are the devil's ideas and no more than devilish treachery, that the sacrament is only the deception and seduction from the clergy, wrong and not
45 holy. . . .

(c) From the confession of Dyonisius of Diest.

[He] has come to Munster by his own decision; he has heard about the gospel which is preached there and so has gone there. . . .

At first the prophet had been an apostle and preached and then he
became a prophet and prophesied and has now been elected by the
50 people as the king from God who will justly administer to everyone and
his name is Johann van Leyden. . . .

The almighty God had said through his prophet that everybody
should be baptised, that it was God's will to cleanse the town and he
who would not convert and do God's will would be punished by God's
55 will. . . .

They destroyed the temples and buildings of Baal and furnished
themselves with the jewels and decorations of the churches.

They do not think much of the sacrament; because they have one
God and he is in heaven. They threw the relics and bones out into the
60 churchyard.

From documents in the Stadtarchiv, Munster.

Questions

★ *a* What 'signs and wonders' (line 11) had happened in Munster?
  b Why would people be attracted to Munster as described by Jacob in
     lines 29–33?
  c Who are meant by 'the heathens and godless' (lines 40–1)? Why
     might they be reluctant to accept all those who were attracted to
     the city?
★ *d* What was the outcome of the rule of the 'king from God' (line 50)?
     How far was this outcome the result of what was said and done at
     Munster as described in these extracts?

8 The Will and Testament of an Anabaptist

My son, hear the instruction of your mother. . . . Behold, I go today the
way of the prophets, apostles, and martyrs, and drink of the cup of
which they have all drunk. I go . . . the way which Christ Jesus, the
eternal Word of the Father, full of grace and truth, the Shepherd of the
5 sheep, who is the Life, Himself went. . . .

So Paul says: 'Thus it pleased the Father, that all whom He
predestinated from eternity, He called, elected, justified and made to be
conformed to the image of His Son.' Our Blessed Saviour also says: 'The
servant is not above his Lord; but it is sufficient for him, that he be like
10 his Lord and Master.' . . . See, my son, here you can hear that no one can
come unto life, except through this way. . . .

Therefore, my child, do not regard the great number, nor walk in
their ways. Remove thy foot far from their paths, for they go to hell, as
sheep unto death. But where you hear of a poor, simple, cast-off little
15 flock which is despised and rejected by the world, join them; for where
you hear of the cross, there is Christ . . . . Flee the shadow of this world;
become united with God; fear Him alone, keep His commandments,

observe all His words, to do them; write them upon the table of your
heart, bind them upon your forehead, speak day and night of His
20   law. . . . Take the fear of the Lord to be your father, and wisdom shall
be the mother of your understanding. . . . Be not ashamed to confess
Him before men; do not fear men; rather give up your life, than to
depart from the truth. If you lose your body, which is earthly, the Lord
your God has prepared you a better one in heaven.
25   Therefore, my child, strive for righteousness unto death, and arm
yourself with the armour of God. Be a pious Israelite, trample under
foot all unrighteousness, the world and all that is in it, and love only that
which is above. Remember that you are not of this world, even as your
Lord and Master was not. Be a faithful disciple of Christ; for none is fit
30   to pray, unless he has become His disciple, and not before. . . . Whatever
you do, do it all to the praise of His name. Honor the Lord in the works
of your hands, and let the light of the Gospel shine through you. Love
your neighbor. Deal with an open, warm heart thy bread to the hungry,
clothe the naked, and suffer not to have anything twofold; for there are
35   always some who lack. Whatever the Lord grants you from the sweat of
your face, above what you need, communicate to those of whom you
know that they love the Lord; and suffer nothing to remain in your
possession until the morrow, and the Lord shall bless the work of your
hands, and give you His blessing for an inheritance. O my son, let your
40   life be conformed to the Gospel, and may the God of peace, sanctify
your soul and body to His praise.

> Anneken Joris, 1539, in G. H. Williams, *The Radical Reformation*,
> 1962, pp. 384–6

Questions

a   What is meant by 'predestinated' and 'elected' (line 7)?
b   In what ways is the recipient of this document urged to 'remember
     that you are not of this world' (line 28)?
★ c   Why was a 'poor, simple, cast-off little flock' (lines 14–15) likely to
         be a group of Anabaptists?
d   In what ways in particular is the recipient urged to let his life 'be
     conformed to the Gospel' (line 40)?

9   An Anabaptist View of the Church

We confess also that God hath, through Christ, chosen, accepted, and
sought a people for Himself, not having spot, blemish, wrinkle, or any
such thing, but pure and holy, as He Himself is holy. . . .
     The children of God, however, become His children through the
5   unifying Spirit. Thus it is evident that the Church is gathered together
by the Holy Spirit: also that she hath being and is kept in being by Him,
and that there is no other Church apart from that which the Holy Spirit
buildeth and gathereth.

Now because it is a testament of the recognition, knowledge, and
10   grace of God, baptism is also, according to the words of Peter, the bond
of a good conscience with God, that is, of those who have recognized
God. The recognition of God, however, cometh, as hath been said, from
hearing the word of the Gospel. Therefore we teach that those who have
heard the word, believed the same, and have recognized God, should be
15   baptized – and not children. . . .

Since then we must be born of God, and are children of Christ and
not of Adam, we must consider carefully how the birth of Christ came
to pass. . . . This birth, however, taketh place in this wise. If the Word is
heard and the same believed, then faith is sealed with the power of God,
20   the Holy Spirit, who immediately reneweth the man and maketh him
live (after he had been dead in sin) in the righteousness that standeth
before God, so that the man is formed a new creature, a new man after
God's likeness, or is renewed therein. Thus, whosoever is born in this
wise, to him belongeth baptism as a bath of rebirth, signifying that he
25   hath entered into the covenant of the grace and knowledge of God. . . .

Thus we say, and must say and confess, that not we but all baptizers
of children have forsaken the Church and community of Christ and
separated themselves and the same. They have fallen away, and are
become so corrupt that they neither know nor recognize what the true
30   Church of Christ is and in what way she proveth herself the Church of
Christ. . . . Thus, we have not turned away from the Church of Christ,
but to it; but we have left the soiled and impure assembly, and would
wish all men did so too. . . .

Governmental authority hath been ordained of God because of the
35   turning aside of the people, in that they turned away from him and
walked according to the flesh. . . . But governmental authority was
given in wrath, and so it can neither fit itself into nor belong to Christ.
Thus no Christian is a ruler and no ruler is a Christian, for the child of
blessing cannot be the servant of wrath. Thus, in Christ, not the
40   temporal, but the spiritual sword, doth rule over men, and so ruleth that
they deserve not the temporal sword, therefore also have no need of it.

Peter Rideman, *An Account of Our Religion, Doctrine, and Faith*,
1540, trans. K.E. Hasenberg, 1950, in J.B. Bruce and
M.M. McLaughlin, *The Portable Renaissance Reader*, 1953,
pp. 661–5

Questions

★   *a*   What argument against infant baptism is put forward in lines 4–8?
Why did the other churches not agree with this?

    b   How does someone become fit to receive baptism 'as a bath of
rebirth' (line 24)?

    c   What explanation does the author give for 'governmental
authority' (line 34)? Why does he argue that 'no Christian is a
ruler and no ruler is a Christian' (line 38)? Why do Christians
'deserve not the temporal sword' (line 41)?

d How far could the teaching of this extract be used to justify the separation of its followers from other men?

10 The Fate of Some Anabaptists

(a) Some they have executed by hanging, some they have tortured with inhuman tyranny, and afterwards choked with cords at the stake. Some they roasted and burned alive. Some they have killed with the sword and given them to the fowls of the air to devour. Some they have cast to the fishes. . . . Others wander about here and there, in want, homelessness and affliction, in mountains and deserts, in holes and caves of the earth. They must flee with their wives and little children from one country to another, from one city to another. They are hated, abused, slandered and lied about by all men.

> Menno Simons, 1529, in R. H. Bainton, *The Reformation of the Sixteenth Century*, 1985, p. 102

(b) No human being was able to take away out of their hearts what they had experienced. . . . The fire of God burned within them. They would die ten deaths rather than forsake the divine truth.

They had drunk of the water which is flowing from God's sanctuary, yea of the water of life. Their tent they had pitched not here upon earth, but in eternity. Their faith blossomed like a lily, their loyalty as a rose, their piety and candor as the flower of the garden of God. The angel of the Lord battled for them that they could not be deprived of the helmet of salvation. Therefore they have borne all torture and agony without fear. The things of this world they counted only as shadows. They were thus drawn unto God that they knew nothing, sought nothing, desired nothing, loved nothing but God alone. Therefore they had more patience in their suffering than their enemies in tormenting them.

> An Anabaptist Chronicle, in R. H. Bainton, *The Reformation of the Sixteenth Century*, 1985, p. 103

(c) An Anabaptist Hymn

Sheep without shepherd running blind
Are scattered into flight.
Our house and home are left behind,
Like birds we fly by night,
And like the birds, naught overhead
Save wind and rain and weather,
In rocks and caves our bed.

We creep for refuge under trees.
They hunt us with the bloodhound.
Like lambs they take us as they please
And hold us roped and strong-bound.

They show us off to everyone
35 As if the peace we'd broken,
As sheep for slaughter looked upon,
As heretics bespoken.

Some in heavy chains have lain
And rotting there have stayed.
40 Some upon the trees were slain,
Choked and hacked and flayed.
Drownings by stealth and drownings plain
For matron and for maid.
Fearlessly the truth they spoke
45 And were not ashamed.
Christ is the way and Christ the life
Was the word proclaimed.
Precious in Thy sight, O God,
The dying of a saint.

50 Our comfort this beneath the rod
Whenever we are faint,
In Thee, O God, in Thee alone
Are earthly peace and rest.
Who hope on Thee, eternally
55 Are sustained and blessed.

R. H. Bainton, *The Reformation of the Sixteenth Century*, 1985 p. 104

Questions

a   Why should Anabaptists have to 'wander about here and there, in want, homelessness and affliction' (lines 5–6)?

b   What made it possible for them, according to the chronicler, to bear 'all torture and agony without fear' (lines 18–19)?

c   What is the hymn-writer implying about the Anabaptists in the lines 'As if the peace we'd broken' (line 35) and 'As heretics bespoken' (line 37)?

★ d   Why did Anabaptists rouse such strong opposition from authorities of all kinds and why were they so willing to accept their fate?

VI Support for Luther

There was a great deal of support for Luther from the beginning, even though some of the most important people who seemed to be on his side at first, such as Erasmus and Zwingli, later changed their minds when they had studied further his ideas and expression.

Others backed Luther because they thought he agreed with them, only to discover that they had misinterpreted his ideas and he strongly disagreed with them. The most notable example of this was the rebellious peasants, whose revolt brought down on their heads one of the most famous of Luther's tirades (see Chapter II, extract 7).

In many places in Germany there was real enthusiasm for Luther and his teaching and Lutheranism quickly became the 'official' religion in many cities and states within the Holy Roman Empire. In these places the correct preaching became an important part of civic life and acceptance of it a test of loyalty (see extracts 8 and 9 below).

The speed with which Lutheranism spread through the Empire is remarkable and owes much to Luther's own personality, but there were several other reasons as well. The spread of the printing press was the most important of these, as it made it possible for Luther's words to be circulated quickly and widely; printers could be certain of making money from something with Luther's name on it, whether or not they agreed with the contents or had any authority to publish it. In addition Luther's position at a well-known university was important. It was customary for students to study for a time at several universities and, as they were often destined for the priesthood (at least before coming into contact with Luther), they were the ideal people to understand and then spread Luther's ideas.

In a different way, the growing criticism of the Catholic church and associated anticlericalism helped to draw people to Luther's teachings, while his belief that the church should be subject to the state combined with national feeling to attract the German princes and encouraged them subsequently to accept Lutheranism as the religion of their states.

However, it must not be forgotten that while these ideas were attractive at first, they did not always become deeply established and by the end of the sixteenth century a number of towns had reverted to Roman Catholicism, partly as a result of the Catholic revival or Counter Reformation, itself in part a consequence of Luther's preaching.

1 Erasmus supports Luther

(a) It has distressed pious minds to hear in the universities scarcely a single discourse about the doctrine of the Gospel; to see those sacred authors, so long approved by the Church, now considered antiquated; to hear in sermons very little about Christ but a great deal about the
5 power of the Pope, and the opinions of recent writers thereon. Every discourse openly manifests self-interest, flattery, ambition, and pretence. Even though Luther has written somewhat intemperately, I think that the blame should rest on these very happenings. Whoever favours the doctrine of the Gospel favours the Roman pontiff, who is the chief
10 herald thereof, although the rest of the bishops are also likewise heralds. We have, in my opinion, a pious pontiff; but in these tempestuous times there are many things of which he is not aware; many things also which even if he wished to do so he could not control.

> Erasmus to Albert of Brandenburg, 19 October 1519, in
> R. L. DeMolen, *Erasmus: Documents of Modern History*, 1973,
> pp. 127–8

(b) I have written recently to Philipp Melanchthon, but in such a
15 manner that I feel as if I had written to Luther by that same letter. I pray that Christ the Almighty will so temper the pen and mind of Luther that he will procure for evangelical piety the greatest possible amount of good, and that he will give to certain people a better understanding – people who seek their own glory by the ignominy of Christ and follow
20 their own profit by abandoning Him. In the camp of those who oppose Luther I perceive many who smack of the world more than of Christ. And yet there are faults on both sides. . . . I should prefer Luther to refrain from these contentions for a little while, and to expound the Gospel simply, without admixture of personal feelings: perhaps his
25 undertaking would succeed better. Just now he is exposing even good literature to an ill-will which is ruinous to us and unprofitable to himself. And there is danger that the corruption of public morality, which all declare requires a public remedy, may, like a pestilence that is stirred up afresh, wax ever more strongly. Not always is the truth to be
30 put forth. And it makes a wide difference in what manner it is put forth.

> Erasmus to Georg Spalatin, 6 July 1520, in R. L. DeMolen,
> *Erasmus: Documents of Modern History*, 1973, p. 128

(c) As to Luther himself, I perceived that the better a man was the less he was Luther's enemy. The world was sick of teaching which gave it nothing but glosses and formulas, and was thirsting after the water of life from the Gospels and Epistles. I approved of what seemed good in
35 his work. I told him in a letter that if he would moderate his language he might be a shining light, and that the Pope, I did not doubt, would be his friend. . .

I have myself simply protested aginst his being condemned before he has been heard in his defence. The penalty for heresy used to be only
40 excommunication. No crime now is more cruelly punished. But how, while there are persons calling themselves bishops and professing to be guardians of the truth, whose moral character is abominable, can it be right to persecute a man of unblemished life, in whose writings distinguished and excellent persons have found so much to admire? The
45 object has been simply to destroy him and his books out of mind and memory, and it can only be done when he is proved wrong by argument and Scripture before a respectable commission that can be trusted.

> Erasmus to Cardinal Lorenzo Campeggio, 6 December 1520, in
> R. L. DeMolen, *Erasmus: Documents of Modern History*, 1973,
> pp. 129–30

Questions

a   How is Erasmus defending Luther to Albert of Brandenburg?

b   Why does Erasmus argue to Spalatin that Luther is both able to do 'the greatest possible amount of good' (lines 17–18) and could 'succeed better' (line 25)?

c   What does Erasmus tell Cardinal Campeggio is the reason for the success of Luther's teaching? Does he think there is any fundamental difference between Luther's teaching and that of the Roman Catholic church?

d   What defence of Luther and criticism of the way he is being treated is Erasmus making to the cardinal?

★ *e*   How did Erasmus' opinion of Luther change? (See Chapter VII, extract 5.)

f   Do you think Erasmus writes more positively about Luther to Spalatin, who could be expected to support Luther, than to Albert and the Cardinal, who were opposed to him?

2 Advice from a Friend

Greeting: I replied from Strasbourg to the letter that you kindly wrote to me recently, and I added at the same time Erasmus' opinion of you, and described his frank and gratifying admiration of your discussion of indulgences. In the meantime I have seen your sermon on Penitence and
5 another on Indulgences and Faith, both in the most obvious opposition to the received customs of our time. I was astounded, in my friendly solicitude, to see you exposing your unprotected body to the dense array of the enemy, even if you do appear to be fully equipped with the arms of truth. You will, I much fear, be attacked with other weapons, and the
10 danger is that the question will be settled by force.

If you will deign to lend an ear to the counsels of one who has had much experience in these matters, I would warn you to adopt the tactics of Sertorius. Believe me, you can undermine gradually what you can never overthrow by force. Your enemies hold a citadel which, as you can see, is protected on every side. Behind a triple line of defense and beyond the range of missiles they are snoring peacefully. Their threefold safety lies in the authority of the pope (that is, of the Church universal), in the potent arm of the despots, and in the persistent support of the universities. . . .

Consequently, I beg of you, lest this noble enterprise of yours come to naught, to resort to a little dissimulation, so that you may get your hook well fixed in your reader before he suspects your object. . . .

Recently I received a book by Silvester Prierius, which he has absurdly enough directed against your treatment of indulgences. If you are going to reply, I would have you do so in prudent language and so reflect the true spirit of Christ as he appears in the Gospels. . . . Then remember that certain kinds of nonsense are frequently better dispelled by a laugh than by laborious effort. Be very careful withal not to attack the pope himself, but lay all the blame on Prierius for his impudent adulation, and for suggesting motives unworthy of the papal dignity, simply in the interests of his own belly. Oppose yourself to the unblushing sycophants, as if you were endeavoring to cut off the opportunity for evil. Where, as you write, you seem to see a chance for them to reply, block the way, so that they cannot reach you to strike back.

But whither am I being carried by the zeal of friendship, as if I were your master and laying down rules for you? Condone my offense, I beg of you. You are not without helpers: Andreas Carlstadt, George Spalatin, John Egranus, and Philip Melanchthon, – the latter a miracle of ability, – to whom, if you communicate your plans, you will publish nothing weak or which can be criticised. But why all this long message from me, except perhaps that it clearly proves my sincere interest in you. . . . Adieu.

Wolfgang Capito, Basel, September 1518, in J. H. Robinson, *Readings in European History*, Vol. II, 1906, pp. 62–4

Questions

a What does the writer mean when he warns that Luther will 'be attacked with other weapons' (line 9) and how could 'the question' 'be settled by force' (line 10)?

b Who were Luther's 'enemies' (line 14)? Why was their position so secure?

c Who were Carlstadt and Spalatin (lines 38–9)? Why should Melanchthon be described as 'a miracle of ability' (lines 39–40)?

★ d How far do you think Luther took notice of Capito's advice?

3   Zwingli's Tribute to Luther, February 1527

Then, I say, there were not a few who knew just as well as you what
religion was about, or even better (though you do not admit it). Indeed,
there are some people whom I have known for the last twelve years
who gave this business attention and moved me to activity. Yet there
5   was no one in all the camps of Israel who dared to throw himself
zealously into the combat; they were so afraid of that monster Goliath,
so feared the menace of so many armed men.

Here indeed you were the only faithful David anointed hereto by the
Lord and furnished likewise with arms. At first you started to argue
10 with them according to their rules and set out your paradoxes [i.e.
Luther's ninety–five theses] to cut the Gordian knot. Soon, however,
casting aside these hindrances, you picked suitable stones from the
heavenly river and flung them so skilfully that you stretched that great
body flat on the open field. Hence faithful souls should never cease
15 energetically singing 'Saul has slain his thousands but David his ten
thousands.' You were that one Hercules who dealt with any trouble that
arose anywhere. You slew the Roman boar and crushed Anteus the son
of earth. Who has set forth more clearly and plainly than you from
apostolic sources the hostility of body and soul? . . . What more? You
20 would have cleansed the Augean stable, if you had had the images
removed, if you had not taught that the body of Christ was supposed to
be eaten in the bread, if you had perceived, by the light of the gospel,
that purgatory is a net for collecting money whereas absolution (what
the gospel calls 'keys') signifies faith, there being but one God with his
25 son Christ Jesus as mediator between God and man. If you had done all
this, not only would you have effected a thorough cleansing but you
would have taken heaven itself on your shoulders.

Huldrych Zwingli, in G. R. Potter, *Huldrych Zwingli: Documents
of Modern History*, 1978, pp. 100–1

Questions

a   For what is Zwingli praising Luther?
b   Explain who or what Zwingli means by 'the Roman boar' (line 17)
'apostolic sources' (line 19) and 'images' (line 20).
★   c   What was the disagreement between Luther and Zwingli about 'the
body of Christ . . . eaten in the bread' (lines 21–2) and on what later
occasion did this subject cause problems between them?
★   d   Do you think that greater agreement between the two men would
have helped the cause of Reform or would it have made little
difference?

4 A German Introduction to *Exsurge Domine*

Ulrich von Hutten, knight, to all Germans: greeting!

Behold Leo X's bull to you, men of Germany. Here he tries once more to stamp out resurgent Christian truth which he attacks and opposes, as our freedom raises its head again after long repression, lest it gain
5 strength and revive for all to see. Shall we not withstand him as he contrives such plots? Shall we not be thoroughly forearmed, by taking public counsel against his intruding further and making headway by means of man's insatiable cupidity and boldness? I ask you by the immortal Christ – when was there a more opportune moment, when
10 did a better occasion present itself as one worthy of bearing the name 'German'? See, everything points to the fact that there is a greater hope than ever before that this tyranny will be wiped out, and this disease find a cure. Dare to attempt it at last, and accomplish it! It is not just Luther who is involved in this business, but whatever the issue, it affects us all;
15 the sword is not thrust at any one individual, but we do public battle. They do not want to be deposed from their tyranny; they do not want their frauds to be detected, their deceits brought to light, their frenzy resisted, their depredations to meet any opposition. This is precisely what they are angry about, and they rail against it so much that they
20 behave with utter lack of dignity. You who see this happening under your nose, what will you do at last? Do you want advice? If you will heed mine, you will surely remember that you are Germans. This alone should be sufficient motive for you to vindicate these things. I am now assuming this risk in your name and the common name, but I do so
25 gladly: first, because I am convinced it is the most fitting thing to do; secondly, I now not only hope, but I am perfectly sure, that you will all sooner or later join me in daring these high deeds. I have made myself responsible for publishing this bull now in the hope that when you read it, you will all be willing to take instruction from a single source.
30 Farewell.

> Ulrich von Hutten, 1520, in I.D.K. Siggins (ed.), *Luther*, 1972, pp. 88–9

Questions

a   What was the purpose of 'Leo X's bull' (line 2)?

b   What grounds does Hutten give for publishing his translation of the bull? How far were his concerns religious and how far were they political?

c   How far would Luther have agreed with the description that the pope was trying 'to stamp out resurgent Christian truth' (line 3)?

★ d   To what extent do Hutten's criticisms of the papacy here reinforce those he made to the Elector of Saxony, also in 1520 (see Chapter I, extract 4)?

5 The Wittenberg Nightingale

First Luther tells us that we all
Inherit sin from Adam's fall,
In evil lust and foul intent
And avid pride our lives are spent;
5   Our hearts are black and unrefined
Our wills to horrid sins inclined,
And God, who judges soul and mind
Has cursed and damned all human kind.
Within our hearts we know this state,
10   Feel burdened with a dreadful weight
Of anguish, fear, bewilderment
That we should be so impotent.
Sure of man's inability
We change pride to humility
15   And then, and only then, we see
The Gospel, sent to make us free,
For in it we find Christ, God's son
Who for us man so much has done,
Fulfilled the law, wiped clean the stain
20   And won God's grace for us again.

Hans Sachs, 1523, in A. G. Dickens, *The German Nation and Martin Luther*, 1974, p. 142

Questions

a   In what way is the poet preaching Lutheran doctrine in lines 15–20? What implicit criticism of Roman Catholic teaching is there in the earlier part of the poem?

★   b   Why could this and similar poems be important in spreading Luther's ideas?

c   Why should the title of this poem seem inappropriate?

6 A Dispute about Luther

Peasant: How marvellous are the works of God! He grants his spirit and grace to humble hearts that put their trust, hope, consolation and faith in him, and he withdraws it from those who trust in their own reason, human fancy and wit. . . .

5   *Erasmus*: I am quite certain that with my publications I have won more favour with the pope's holiness, all the cardinals and bishops, and also other princes, than ever did Luther and all his company who have called down upon themselves envy, hatred and persecution – afflictions which all my life I have managed to avoid.

10   *Peasant*: My dear Erasmus, we are well aware that you are careful not to tangle with foxes. The truth, which has its own effect and which respects neither small nor great, high estate or low, has never found

much thanks among the hierarchies and powers. It has always attracted
persecution and envy, and upon its followers it has always inflicted that
15 cross that you don't much like. Your nature and quality drive you rather
to worship Antichrist than to live on herbs. . . .
John Fabri, a theologian and pamphleteer: What, you Lutheran heretic, still
here? When will you recant? What moves you to destroy your soul by
following Luther? You are not content with seducing yourself: you
20 must teach your neighbours disobedience too. By my troth, it will not
go well with you.
Peasant: We have the Word of God, the holy gospel – in that we believe
and not in the chatter that comes from your idol in Rome. For we have
now learned that that is nothing but lies, deceit, trickery, robbery and
25 usury – just to get our money.
Fabri: Think you, if the holy fathers, the popes and the Councils were to
do an injustice, that so many holy fathers would have applauded and
approved? Moreover, your forefathers have for hundreds of years
believed those things which you and your Lutheran rabble now profess
30 to despise in your disobedience to the See of Rome. You'd do better to
follow the example of your parents.
Peasant: That I deny. . . My faith stands not upon my parents but upon
the Word of God, on the consolation and promise of Christ announced
in the holy gospel. While I build upon that, I stand upon unmoving,
35 solid ground and am sure that I cannot err.
Fabri: You vile louts, you all want to be Lutherans now, you need
whipping. . . . You German rogues, you never do good unless a foreign
nation be brought in to teach you the faith and also how to prove
obedient to the See of Rome.
40 *Peasant*: Ah, Faber, away with you. All this pulling of cruel faces. We
peasants no longer fear you and your Antichrist at Rome. We know
whence you come. The rulers of this world, being pious, will not
compel us to leave off the Word of God upon which depends our
salvation, the greatest treasure we have. But if, for lack of understanding
45 or from mischievous knavery, they were to try, we will first, in all
humility, ask them to allow us the Word. And thereafter, with the
power and grace of the Lord God, we shall be strong enough to be more
obedient to him than to you apostate blasphemers. And we shall let no
one take the holy Word of the gospel away from us, and upon that we
50 wager our lives and all we have.

From an anonymous pamphlet, 1524, in G. R. Elton, *Renaissance
and Reformation*, 1976, pp. 193–5

Questions

★ *a* By the time this pamphlet was written, Erasmus had made public
his disagreement with Luther. What reason does this, hostile, writer
give for Erasmus' action? What other reasons might Erasmus have
had?

b   The Peasant represents the ordinary follower of Luther. What 'things' did he 'now profess to despise in [his] disobedience to the See of Rome' (lines 29–30)?

c   What were 'Councils' (line 26) and why were they important? Who was 'Antichrist' (line 41)?

*   d   Was the Peasant justified in his claim that 'the rulers of this world, being pious, will not compel us to leave off the Word of God' (lines 42–3)?

e   How far does the Peasant seem to you to make out a convincing case for continuing to be a Lutheran?

7   The Handbook of the Evangelical Burgher

Those only are the good works commanded by God which are done in faith and out of love and not for the sake of salvation or temporal gain, but only to the praise and honor of God and for the purpose of doing some good for one's neighbor. . . . We Christians should remember the
5   young man who asked Christ what should be done as good works so that eternal life might be inherited. We do not find that the Lord said: 'Go forth and buy many masses, say many long prayers, go on a pilgrimage, endow churches, altars, towers, bells, expensive paintings, burn many candles.' He also did not say: 'Have no wife, remain a virgin,
10   do not eat this or that food, fast and celebrate on this or that day, confess to a priest the secrets of your heart, go into a cloister, wear a cowl and the clothes of pharisees, or be buried in a gray cowl, and various similar works so highly valued by men today.' Rather Christ said: 'You know the commandment well,' and told him the commandment to love his
15   neighbor: 'If you will inherit eternal life, keep the commandment and love your neighbor as yourself.' And when the youth thought that he had already done that, the Lord said to him: 'If you will be perfect (for one thing still remains for you to do), go and sell what you have and give it to the poor.' He did not say: 'Go and give what you have to the
20   learned theologians, the religious, the monasteries, the high cathedral chapters, abbots, priests, monks, and nuns so that they will pray and perform works of reconciliation for you.' No, he rather said: 'Give to the poor who need such help, and take up the cross and follow me.' Now that is for sure the true work, if done out of faith and love, that
25   brings us to eternal life.

Arnd von Aich, c. 1530, in S. E. Ozment, *The Reformation in the Cities*, 1975, pp. 161–2

Questions

a   Why had people for so long been encouraged to 'buy many masses' (line 7)?

b   Who are meant by 'the religious' (line 20) and why were 'works of reconciliation' (line 22) considered necessary?

★   *c*   Explain the various ways in which Luther had gone against the traditional teaching of the Catholic church, as shown in this extract.

8 Protestant Preaching

(a) I wish to have no freedoms beyond those of other Christians and laymen. I fully recognize the authority of the magistracy over myself as over any layman and wish to give it every possible obedience, whether it pertain to honor, body or goods, as I and every man am obligated by
5   divine law to do. I desire to be punished when I deserve it. I ask only that I be permitted to do what God has given me the right to do, and which none [but he] can deny, to earn my living by serving my neighbor [as a priest]. Good, divine preaching cannot be harmed by my marriage, regardless of what any law says. Saint Paul wanted even
10   bishops, or preachers in high positions of leadership, to have honorable wives.

> Martin Bucer, 1523, in S. E. Ozment, *The Reformation in the Cities,* 1975, pp. 147–8

(b) An Instruction to All Preachers on How the Gospel of Christ Is to Be Preached and Taught in Constance, issued by the Magistracy, February 1524

[The clergy were henceforth to preach only the gospel] according to true Christian understanding, without any admixture of human traditions that have no basis in the holy biblical Scriptures . . . and
15   especially to omit all fables, useless little things, and matters of dispute which Christians can just as well do without, together with whatever might lead them into error or turn them against their magistrates, preaching only what truly serves the honor of God and quiets consciences, building up the love of God and one's fellowmen.

> In S. E. Ozment, *The Reformation in the Cities*, 1975, p. 149

(c) The Installation of a Court Preacher at Marburg, August 1525
20   He shall be our preacher, obligated by his office to stand in God's place and proclaim clearly and purely to us and all men the word of God and the holy Gospel. This he shall do according to true Christian understanding on the basis of Scripture and with an eye to planting every good among us. He shall also be prepared to travel hither and yon
25   and visit other pastors and otherwise let himself be sent and employed as we desire and command. And he shall do with God's grace all that is expected of a pious Christian preacher obligated by Scripture and his office.

> In S. E. Ozment, *The Reformation of the Cities*, 1975, pp. 134–5

Questions

★   *a*   What is there in Bucer's statement to indicate that he was not a Roman Catholic and might be a follower of Luther?

b   Why was it regarded as important in Constance not to include 'any admixture of human traditions' (lines 13–14) in preaching?

c   Why might the authorities at Marburg want their preacher to 'visit other pastors' (line 25)?

d   From all these three extracts, what qualities were needed to be a successful preacher in a German city in the 1520s?

9   Civic Religion

(a) Oath of civic loyalty in Goslar, 1528

If the council and the said city should find themselves in distress and adversity as a result of the abolition of the Mass and other ceremonies, or on account of the Holy Gospel (which is now preached as it should be in all its purity and clarity), I promise to show myself obedient, putting my
5   life and goods at the service of your noble council and of the town of Goslar, as long as I shall be a citizen and inhabitant. May God help me: He and his Holy Gospel.

> H. Holscher, *Die Geschichte der Reformation in Goslar*, 1902, in
> A. G. Dickens, *The German Nation and Martin Luther*, 1974, p. 188

(b) Ordinance for Brandenburg/Nurnberg, 1533

A church order is here conceived and brought together not in the belief that by the observance of such prescribed works men repent their sins
10   and earn God's grace, for only Christ can redeem man's sin, and he has already earned God's grace for us. Rather this church order is prescribed in the belief that a true and orderly discipline of the congregation of the church provides both the occasion and the motivation to attend the preaching of God's word more diligently and to receive the sacrament
15   more earnestly.

> Johannes Brenz, in S. E. Ozment, *The Reformation in the Cities*,
> 1975, pp. 154–5

(c) To the Town Council of Augsburg

Grace and peace in Christ. Honorable, wise, and dear friends! I have heard both of your preachers, together with others, and have done all in my power for them, as they themselves will tell you. At last, thank God, we are at one on all things, so far as human power can tell; wherefore I
20   kindly and humbly beg you, as much as you can, to make our union strong and permanent. I have earnestly prayed and admonished your ministers to do the same, that we may not only teach the same doctrine with our mouths but also trust one another from the bottom of our hearts, eradicating all offence as true love is bound to do. If our
25   agreement please you and your ministers, kindly inform us, as we shall tell you and others how we are pleased with the union. Then we will have it publicly printed, to the praise of God and the hurt of the devil

and his members. Amen. The Father of all comfort and peace strengthen
and guide your hearts with us in the right knowledge of his dear Son
30   our Lord Jesus Christ, in whom all the riches of wisdom and knowledge
are hidden. Amen.

Your devoted Martin Luther, May 1536. Letter in P. Smith, *The
Life and Letters of Martin Luther, 1911, pp. 294–5

Questions

★   *a*   Why might the town of Goslar find itself 'in distress and adversity
as a result of the abolition of the Mass' (lines 1–2)?

b   What is the significance of the phrase 'He and his Holy Gospel'
(line 7)?

c   What is meant by 'a church order' (line 8)?

d   In what way can 'a true and orderly discipline of the congregation'
(line 12) provide 'the motivation to attend the preaching of God's
word' (lines 13–14)?

e   In what sense was there to be a 'union' (line 20) between Luther and
the town of Augsburg?

★   *f*   Why did towns and cities which accepted Lutheran preaching often
find it necessary to make this a matter of civic obedience?

10   Theological Training at Wittenberg

**Statutes of the collegiate faculty of theology in the University of
Wittenberg, drawn up in the year 1533**

I On the nature of the doctrine
As in the churches throughout our jurisdiction and in the grammar
schools, so in the university the special governance and censorship of
doctrine is weaker than it ought to be. We therefore wish that the pure
5   doctrine of the gospel, in agreement with the confession which we
presented to the Emperor Charles at Augsburg in 1530, the doctrine
which we stated with certainty to be the true and perpetual consensus of
the catholic Church of God, should be devoutly and faithfully set
forward, preserved, and propagated. . . .
10   *II* There shall be four permanent full-time lecturers, to be subject to the
rector of the university, admitted by the judgement of this collegiate
faculty, and having the public qualification of the doctor's degree
conferred either by this or another university. These four are to be the
college of this faculty, and to administer the affairs and actions of this
15   college by common counsel, and above all faithfully to protect concord
in doctrine, as it is fitting for those in authority in the Church to do. But
if any of them has received his doctor's degree in another university, he
shall not be received into this college unless his erudition and experience
in public disputation has first been explored. And all who are received,

20   whether they have received their doctor's degree here or elsewhere, are
to promise that they will faithfully pursue and demand this consensus of
doctrine.
III Exposition of some book of the Old Testament is always to be
offered by one of these, and exposition of a book of the New Testament
25   by another. Expositions of the Epistle of St Paul to the Romans, the
Gospel of John, Psalms, Genesis, and Isaiah are to be repeated most
often. For these books are best able to teach students the major points of
Christian doctrine. Meanwhile, one of the professors is also to expound
the book of Augustine *On the Spirit and the Letter*, so that the students
30   may see that the doctrine of our churches also possesses the testimony of
learned fathers. And in these expositions the simple truth is to be
candidly taught in accordance with God's command, and rightly and
properly explained in a clear manner of speech. . . .
VIII There is also to be some selection in admitting those who seek
35   degrees. As Paul teaches that hands are not to be laid indiscriminately on
anyone, so not all are to be granted these qualifications, which in fact
can be awarded with good conscience only to those suitable.
Accordingly, those who are fascinated with distorted opinions which
fight against the doctrine of our churches are not to be admitted to a
40   degree. Similarly, no disreputable persons are to be admitted. . . . But let
the character of those who are admitted to degrees be modest and chaste,
as Paul requires of bishops. For this reason, we also command that
upright married persons who devote themselves to ecclesiastical teaching
are to be admitted to all degrees. Permission is also to be granted for
45   upright men who were celibate before graduation afterwards to contract
a marriage according to Christian doctrine. Permission is also to be
granted for one whose spouse has died to marry again according to
Christian doctrine. We do not impose upon anyone the old laws and
bonds concerning celibacy. . . . Teachers of theology are rather to
50   understand that marriage has been ordained by the marvellous and
ineffable counsel of God for the mutual society and assistance of the
human race and for preserving the Church. And they are to recognise
that this way of life is pleasing to God, and is a school of many virtues
for the good.

Statutes, 1533, in I. D. K. Siggins (ed.), *Luther*, 1972, pp. 135–8

Questions

a   What is meant by 'the catholic Church' as in line 8?
b   Who was responsible for 'the confession . . . presented . . . at
Augsburg in 1530' (lines 5–6) and what was its purpose?
c   Why was it so necessary to examine the 'erudition and experience'
(line 18) of those educated at other universities before allowing
them to teach theology at Wittenberg?

    d   Why should a Lutheran university lay particular stress on teaching about Paul's Epistle to the Romans and the other books mentioned in paragraph III?

★   *e*   Why had students previously been obliged to be celibate to study at a university? Why was ability not to be the sole criterion for the awarding of a degree but suitability (see lines 36–7)?

VII   Opposition to Luther

Opposition to Luther came from all sides and on both religious and political grounds. The immediate reaction to Luther's attack on indulgences came, not surprisingly, in the name of the powerful salesman Tetzel. Then, once Charles V had been elected Holy Roman Emperor and it was no longer so important to the pope to keep the support of the Elector of Saxony, Luther was excommunicated. These attacks were essentially theological but, at the pope's request, they were followed by Charles's summons to Luther to appear before the Diet at Worms and his condemnation and ban there.

The theological attack intensified over the years as it began to come from what might be described as the religious 'left' as well as the 'right'. Erasmus, on the right, found himself increasingly unsympathetic to Luther and soon voiced this opinion, even though it brought scorn and accusations about his preference for a quiet life from some of Luther's supporters. From the left came opposition from Zwingli, whose initial support Luther lost because he was too conservative to please Zwingli. This was even more true of the real radicals, represented here by Muntzer, but also typified by Karlstadt and others who wanted to go much further than Luther and could not understand his reluctance to destroy completely the framework of an organised church.

The decrees of the Council of Trent might seem an unexpected inclusion here, but they were mostly drawn up before 1555, the traditional end-date for the German Reformation, and they also crystalise and formalise the differences between the Catholic church and Luther. A number of these decrees were specifically aimed at excluding Lutherans, and all other kinds of Protestant, from the universal church, once the failure of the Diet of Regensburg in 1541 had finally convinced everyone that reconciliation between Catholics and Lutherans was impossible. This was also the stage at which Charles V decided that he could only deal with the problem of Lutheranism by force, even though he was not able to follow up his subsequent military success with the elimination of heresy from the Empire.

1   Tetzel's Countertheses

1. *Our Lord Jesus Christ,* who wanted the sacraments of the new law to be binding upon all men after his passion and ascension, also wanted to teach all men those sacraments before his passion through his own plainest preaching. Therefore anyone who says: *When Christ preached,*

5   *'be penitent'*, he intended by this interior penitence and the exterior mortification
     of the flesh, in such a way that he cannot also teach or conclude that the
     sacrament of penance, and its component parts confession and
     satisfaction, are equally obligatory – he is in error.
     2. Indeed, it is no help if *inner repentance* also *produces outward*
10   *mortification,* if confession and satisfaction are not also present by deed
     or by vow. . . .
     6. None the less, one is bound as long as one lives to grieve inwardly by
     act or by habit, and always to detest the sin remitted, and not to be
     without fear about the propitiation of sins.
15   7. This penalty, imposed because of sins regretted and confessed, the
     pope is able to remit entirely through indulgences, whether it is imposed
     by himself or by a priest, whether *by his own authority or by canon,* or
     even if it is demanded by divine justice – to contradict this is to err.
     8. But even if every penalty incurred as retribution for sins may be
20   remitted through indulgences, yet it is a mistake to think that therefore a
     penalty which is curative and preservative is removed, since no time of
     release is offered against that penalty. . . .
     13. Indeed, just as God possesses the keys of authority, and Christ the
     keys of supremacy, so the Christian priest has the keys of administration.
25   Therefore anyone who says that the pope or even the least of priests has
     no power over guilt except by *approving* or *declaring* is in error.
     14. In fact, he errs who does not believe that the least Christian priest has
     more power over sin than the whole synagogue formerly possessed.
     15. Furthermore, he errs who thinks that Christ cannot remit sins or save
30   a man without priestly confession, *approbation* or *declaration* by means of
     his own key's superiority, in whose exercise he has not bound his power
     to the sacraments. . . .
     93. For those who have confessed and are contrite and have been
     released through indulgences, *peace, peace* is a fact since every retributive
35   penalty has been taken away – to contradict is to err.
     94. But the remnants of one's sins – one's proclivity and ease of relapse –
     remain; to heal them, so that they do not burst forth in new sins,
     curative penalties, *crosses* and castigations are demanded.
     95. Thus when pardons have been duly obtained, there is *peace, peace*
40   from past retributive penalties. But there remains *the cross, the cross* as a
     warning against future penalties – whoever denies this has no
     understanding, but errs and raves.
            Dr Konrad Koch, January 1518, in I. D. K. Siggins (ed.), *Luther,*
            1972, pp. 60–1
     [The phrases in italics are directly quoted from Luther's ninety-five
     theses by Dr Koch, who drew up this document for Tetzel.]

Questions

a   What are meant by 'mortification of the flesh' (lines 5–6) and
       'canon' (line 17)?

b   What error is Luther accused of in article 7?

c   What papal power has Luther challenged, according to article 13, and why did this seem a particularly serious error?

d   How, according to article 15, has Luther attacked the power of priests?

e   Why do you think the author suggested that Luther 'errs and raves' (line 42)?

2   *Exsurge Domine*

Leo, bishop, servant of the servants of God. . . . Arise, Lord, and judge your cause! Be mindful of the trespasses against you which are committed every day by foolish men. . . and when you were about to ascend to the Father you committed the care, government, and
5 administration of this vineyard to Peter, its only head and your vicar, and to his successors as the image of the Church Triumphant. A roaring boar of the forest is trying to devastate it, a single wild beast is devouring it. . . .

For a long time now we have heard from the reliable testimony of
10 worthy men and widespread public report something that we are scarcely able to express without anguish and agony of soul. Indeed truly – oh grief! – we have seen and read with our own eyes many and various errors, some of them already condemned by the councils and rulings of our predecessors. . . . That this should have happened [in
15 Germany] is all the more painful to us because both we and our predecessors have always borne love for that nation in our hearts. . . . Therefore, for the sake of the responsibility of the pastoral office we bear, entrusted to us by divine grace, we can by no means tolerate the pestilential poison of the aforesaid errors any longer. . . .
20 Above all, since these stated errors and many others are contained in the books or writings of Martin Luther, we similarly condemn, reprove, and totally reject the said books and all the writings of the said Martin. . . . We repeat, we want them condemned, reproved, and rejected for all time, forbidding each and every faithful Christian, man or woman, in
25 the power of holy obedience and under the threat of every punishment, to presume to read . . . or defend such writings, books, sermons, or broadsheets . . . or presume in any way to retain them in their homes or in any other place, public or private. Rather, immediately upon publication of this decree, they are to be searched out diligently,
30 wherever they are. . . and publicly and solemnly burnt in the presence of clergy and people. . . .

As for Martin himself, dear God!, what have we neglected, what have we not done, what fatherly love have we omitted in order to recall him from his errors? For . . .[we] invited him . . . to come here . . . . Had he
35 done so, he would certainly (we believe) have changed his heart and acknowledged his errors; and he would not have found in the Roman

curia as many errors as he so severely censures, . . . and in a clearer light we should have taught him that the holy Roman pontiffs, our predecessors, whom he injuriously impugns without any moderation, never erred in the canons and rulings which he is trying to erode. . . .

40

We therefore wholeheartedly exhort and beseech Martin himself and all his adherents, patrons and protectors . . . that they cease disturbing the peace of this Church for which the Saviour prayed so urgently to the Father, and abstain completely from the pernicious errors we have named; and if they comply effectively . . . they will discover in us a response of fatherly love and a flowing spring of gentleness and mercy.

45

Nevertheless, from now on we command the said Martin for the time being to desist altogether from preaching.

Pope Leo X, 1520, in I. D. K. Siggins (ed.), *Luther*, 1972, pp. 72–4

Questions

★   *a*   Why is the document entitled *Exsurge Domini*?

    b   What justification does the pope give for his power to deal with Luther? Why should he describe Luther as 'a roaring boar' (lines 6–7)?

★   *c*   Do you think that the German people would generally have agreed that the popes had 'always borne love' for their nation 'in our hearts' (line 16)?

★   *d*   From his previous experience, do you think Luther would have changed his opinions if he had visited Rome again?

    e   Why should the pope order Luther to stop preaching only 'for the time being' (lines 47–8)? What had to be done when Luther ignored this command?

3   Charles V's Speech at the Diet of Worms

You know that I am a descendant of the Most Christian Emperors of the great German people, of Catholic Kings of Spain, of the Archdukes of Austria and the Dukes of Burgundy. All of these, their whole life long, were faithful sons of the Roman Church. They were the defenders at all times of the Catholic Faith, its sacred ceremonies, decrees, and ordinances, and its holy rites, to the honour of God: they were at all times concerned for the propagation of the faith and the salvation of souls. After their deaths they left, by natural law and heritage, these holy Catholic rites, for us to live by and die by, following their example. And so until now I have lived, by the grace of God, as a true follower of these our ancestors.

5

10

I am, therefore, resolved to maintain everything which these my forebears have established to the present, and especially that which my predecessors ordered as much at the Council of Constance as at other Councils. It is certain that a single monk must err if his opinion is contrary to that of all Christendom. According to his [Luther's] opinion the whole of Christendom has been in error for a thousand years, and is

15

continuing still more so in that error in the present. To settle this matter
I have resolved to stake upon this course my dominions and my
20 possessions, my body and my blood, my life and soul. It would be a
disgrace for me and for you, the noble and renowned German nation,
appointed by peculiar privilege and singular pre-eminence to be the
defenders and protectors of the Catholic Faith, as well as a perpetual
stain upon ourselves and our posterity, if in this our day and generation,
25 not only heresy but even the suspicion of heresy or the diminution of
our Christian religion were due to our negligence.

    After the impudent reply which Luther gave yesterday in the
presence of us all, I now declare that I regret having delayed so long the
proceedings against the aforementioned Luther and his false doctrine. I
30 have now resolved never again, under any circumstances, to hear him.
He is to be escorted home immediately . . . with due regard for the
stipulations of his safe-conduct. He is not to preach or seduce the people
with his evil doctrine and not to incite them to rebellion.

    As I have said above, I am resolved to act and proceed against him as
35 a notorious heretic. I ask you to declare yourselves in this affair as good
Christians, and to keep the promise you made to me.

    James Atkinson, *The Trial of Luther*, 1971, pp. 177–8 in Martyn
    Rady, *The Emperor Charles V*, 1988, pp. 99–100

Questions

a   Why does Charles say that Luther, 'a single monk' (line 15) must be
    wrong?
b   What justification does Charles give for acting against Luther?
★ c   Why had Charles 'delayed so long' (line 28) in dealing with Luther?
d   Explain 'the stipulations of his safe-conduct' (line 32). What penalty
    was imposed on Luther?
★ e   Why did the penalty prove so ineffective in practice?

4   The Edict of the Diet of Worms, 1521

1. We, Charles V, by God's grace Roman emperor elect, ever august,
king of Germany, Spain [etc.], salute and tender our gracious good
wishes to each and all of the electors, princes, – both spiritual and
secular, – prelates, counts, barons, knights, . . . and all other beloved and
5   faithful subjects of ours. . . .
2. It pertains to our office of Roman emperor, to take care that no stain
or suspicion of heresy should contaminate our holy faith within the
Roman Empire, or, if heresy had already begun, to extirpate it with all
necessary diligence, prudence, and discretion, as the case might
10 demand. . . .
4. Whereas certain heresies have sprung up in the German nation within
the last three years, which were formerly condemned by the holy
councils and papal decrees . . . should we permit them to become more

deeply rooted, or, by our negligence, tolerate and bear with them, our
15   conscience would be greatly burdened, and the future glory of our name
would be covered by a dark cloud in the auspicious beginnings of our
reign.

5. Since now without doubt it is plain to you all how far these errors and
heresies depart from the Christian way, which a certain Martin Luther,
20   of the Augustine order, has sought violently and virulently to introduce
and disseminate within the Christian religion and its established order,
especially in the German nation . . . [the] mighty dissolution and pitiable
downfall of good morals, and of the peace and the Christian faith, will
result. . . .

25   9. And although, after the delivery of the papal bull and final
condemnation of Luther, we proclaimed the bull in many places in the
German nation . . . nevertheless Martin Luther has taken no account of
it, nor lessened nor revoked his errors, nor sought absolution from his
Papal Holiness or grace from the holy Christian Church. . .

30   25. Accordingly, in view of all these considerations and the fact that
Martin Luther still persists obstinately and perversely in maintaining his
heretical opinions, and consequently all pious and Godfearing persons
abominate and abhor him as one mad or possessed by a demon, . . . we
have declared and made known that the said Martin Luther shall
35   hereafter be held and esteemed by each and all of us as a limb cut off
from the Church of God, an obstinate schismatic and manifest
heretic. . . .

27. We order and command each and all of you, as you owe fidelity to
us and the Holy Empire . . . [that] you shall refuse to give the aforesaid
40   Martin Luther hospitality, lodging, food or drink; neither shall any one,
by word or deed, secretly or openly, succor or assist him. . . .

29. Consequently we command you, each and all, under the penalties
already prescribed, that henceforth no one shall dare to buy, sell, read,
preserve, copy, print, or cause to be copied or printed, any books of the
45   aforesaid Martin Luther, condemned by our holy father the pope as
aforesaid, or any other writings in German or Latin hitherto composed
by him, since they are foul, harmful, suspected, and published by a
notorious and stiffnecked heretic.

> J.H. Robinson, *Readings in European History,* Vol. II, 1906,
> pp. 83–8

Questions

a   Why is Charles described as 'Roman emperor elect' (line 1)?
b   What is meant by describing Luther as 'of the Augustine order'
(line 20)?
c   What grounds does Charles give for the need to take action against
Luther in paragraphs 2, 4 and 5?
d   How could Luther have 'sought absolution' (line 28) and why was
he never likely to do so?

★ *e* Why did the emperor's orders in paragraphs 27 and 29 fail to solve the problem posed by Luther?

5 Erasmus' Criticism of Luther

(a) Each side pushes me and reproaches me. My silence against Luther is interpreted as consent, while the Lutherans accuse me of having deserted the gospel out of timidity. Luther's abusiveness can be condoned only on the ground that perhaps our sins deserve to be scourged with scorpions. . . . I cannot be other than I am, and cannot but execrate dissension. I cannot but love peace and concord. I see how much easier it is to start than to assuage a tumult. . . .

I do not deny that I seek peace wherever possible. I believe in listening to both sides with open ears. I love liberty. I will not, I cannot serve any faction. I have said that all of Luther's teaching cannot be suppressed without suppressing the gospel; but because I favoured Luther at first I do not see that I am called upon to approve everything he has said since.

Erasmus, 1523, in B. M. G. Reardon, *Religious Thought in the Reformation*, 1981, p. 39

(b) I do not object generally to the evangelical doctrines, but there is much in Luther's teachings which I dislike. He runs everything which he touches into extravagance. True, Christendom is corrupt and needs the rod, but it would be better, in my opinion, if we could have the pope and the princes on our side. . . . Clement was not opposed to reform, but when I urged that we should meet him half-way nobody listened. The violent party carries all before it. They tear the hoods off monks who might as well have been left in their cells. Priests are married, and images are torn down. I would have had religion purified without destroying authority. Licence need not be given to sin. Practices grown corrupt by long usage might be gradually corrected without throwing everything into confusion. Luther sees certain things to be wrong, and in flying blindly at them causes them more harm than he cures. Order human beings as you will, there will still be faults enough, and there are remedies worse than the disease. . . . Would that Luther had tried as hard to improve popes and princes as to expose their faults. . . .

You are anxious that Luther shall answer me with moderation. Unless he write in his own style, the world will say we are in connivance. Do not fear that I shall oppose evangelical truth. I left many faults in him unnoticed lest I should injure the Gospel. I hope mankind will be the better for the acrid medicines with which he has dosed them. Perhaps we needed a surgeon who would use knife and cautery. Carlstadt and he are going so fast that Luther himself may come to regret popes and bishops. . . . The devil is a clever fellow. Success like Luther's might spoil the most modest of men.

Erasmus, Letter to Philip Melanchthon, from Basle, 10 December 1524, in R. L. DeMolen, *Erasmus: Documents of Modern History*, 1973, pp. 149–50

Questions

a   By using the phrase 'on our side' (line 18), Erasmus implies that he and Luther have the same aim. What does the passage suggest that this aim was?

★   b   Why does Erasmus find his own position so difficult?

c   What is Erasmus' chief criticism of Luther? How far was this justified?

d   Why does Erasmus not wish to be answered 'with moderation' (line 30) by Luther?

e   Who was Carlstadt (line 36)? What does Erasmus mean by the sentence about Carlstadt and Luther?

6   A Radical Attack on Luther

To the diligent father and lord, Frederick, Elector of the beloved land of Saxony.

    The unalloyed upright fear of God with the unconquerable Spirit of godly wisdom, in place of my greetings! Since sheer necessity demands
5   that all unfaith should be openly confronted – unfaith which hitherto has assumed the guise of the Christian Church and will now be displayed in the lying shape of carnal and fictitious kindness – by God's command, I am (as Ezekiel says) set before a wall of wretched, corrupt Christianity, which is not merely, as some imagine, to be mildly
10   rebuked, but is even to be torn up completely by the roots, as indeed God in a fitting manner has partly done in some places. Now, however, it is the godless theologians whom Satan drives to their downfall as before it was the monks and priests, for they have betrayed their guile by mocking the Holy Spirit of Christ most contemptuously and
15   denouncing him as a devil in many of the elect, as the lying Luther now does in the scandalous letter against me which he has sent to the Dukes of Saxony, where he blasts forth so grimly and maliciously without any brotherly warning, like some splendid tyrant. Therefore I pray you, for God's sake, to consider earnestly what a ludicrous situation would arise,
20   were I to requite him for his slander, which I am not inclined to do, yet since it has offended many godly men from foreign lands and cities who have heeded my teaching, such slander can hardly be left unanswered.

    I therefore loyally beg that Your Excellency will not prevent or forbid me from serving, preaching, or writing to poor Christendom to
25   avoid the new risk that Christianity may be distorted again under Luther's label, and afterwards restored to unity only with difficulty.

    In short, this is my earnest intention: I preach the sort of Christian faith which does not harmonise with Luther, but which is identical in all

the hearts of the elect upon earth (Psalm 67). . . I have promised my dear
30 lord, Duke John your brother, to submit my books for examination
before printing, but I submit not merely to the venomous and pompous
judgement of the scribes, but even to him who reckons the coming of
faith to the crushed heart. Accordingly, if you will be my gracious lord
and prince, then I will let this Christian faith go forth, in the clear light
35 of day before the whole world, both in speech and writing, and make it
known with all devotion. But if this plea receives no satisfaction from
Your Excellency, then you will have to take account of the aversion and
despair of the common folk against you. . . For the people have pinned
great hopes on you, and God has granted you foresight in advance of
40 other lords and princes. But if you abuse it in this case, then it will be
said of you: 'See, here is a man who was not willing to have God as his
defence, but has abandoned himself to worldly arrogance.'

Thomas Muntzer, a sincere bondsman of God, 1524, in
I. D. K. Siggins (ed.), *Luther*, 1972, pp. 108–9

Questions

★ *a* Who was Thomas Muntzer? Why had he quarrelled with Luther?
   b What did Muntzer mean by 'the Christian church' (line 6)?
   c How does Muntzer suggest that 'Satan drives' theologians 'to their
       downfall' (line 12)?
   d Why does Muntzer think 'Christianity may be distorted again
       under Luther's label' (lines 25–6)?
★ *e* From the tone of this letter, do you think the Elector of Saxony was
       likely to be sympathetic to Muntzer? What other reasons had he for
       supporting Luther?

7 A Friendly Exegesis

To that learned man, Martin Luther, his revered brother in the Lord:
Grace and peace from the Lord.

You have compelled us, most learned Luther, really quite unwillingly
to write this *Exegesis*, in which we have taken you up with somewhat
5 greater freedom than before but without any reproach at all. For I have
always respected you so much that I could not have respected a father
more . . . and I shall not stop respecting you – unless you stubbornly
refuse to bring your resistance to the truth to an end. . . . Once you used
to search the Scriptures diligently, and whatever you uncovered, you
10 confessed and defended before all men and against every sort of enemy.
In all this, there was a strain of bitterness, unbearable to your enemies,
but which we on our part swallowed for a while, during the early stages
of the affair; and as your opponents argued back with daily increasing
sharpness, your own unwillingness to endure it also grew and drove you
15 in an opposite direction, to the point where you now admit not a few of
the very things which you were condemning in the enemy a little while

before. Once you wished that everything should be subject to the judgements of the Church; but now, if the things that are written and said about you are true, you advise whoever you can that our opinion
20 about the Eucharist should not even reach the churches. . . . Once you used to condemn the papists' frenzy and slaughtering; now you advise the princes and their class, even in the absence of the ring-leaders, to rage even more tyrannically, not to say madly, against the wretched slaves with flame and sword, laying waste and slaying not only the rioters, but
25 also innocent masses who only believe that what they see is true. . . . I shall speak plainly. You hope that in return for the efforts you are now exerting, in which you leave natural eating of flesh behind you and are converted into living flesh in a mystery by the power of the divine Spirit – I am afraid to say you hope that when you produce these
30 marvellous and magnificent works, a smokescreen will be stirred up by them which will so capture and hold the attention of both princes and insurgents that they will say: 'The Lord's body must not be taken completely away from the Supper!' But you hope in vain. For you will never get anything than that the body of Christ is present, whether in
35 the Supper or in the minds of the godly, simply and solely by contemplation, and as we progress we shall bring to light all the illusions. . . . And even though we have no desire at all to diminish that authority, yet if there is no other way, we must detract from it a little. My voice has directed these appeals to you from my heart. Your
40 erudition, power and acumen are known and respected by us; but at the same time, we also know the truth. If for any reason you persist in obscuring, or at least obstructing, the truth, we shall deal with you fearlessly. . . .

Be sure that we shall always revere you most deeply if you in your
45 turn continue to be what you hear, namely, *katharos* – that is pure, clean, untainted by self-esteem, and counting as less than nothing the foul abuse of your advisers. Again farewell, and fear not.

Zurich, April 1, 1527. H. Zwingli, yours from the heart, as long as sincerity of the heart and zeal for the truth remain yours.

I. D. K. Siggins, Luther (ed.), 1972, pp. 101–4

Questions

a What is meant by 'Exegesis' (line 4)?
b What grounds does Zwingli give for his original respect for Luther and what reservations has he had from the beginning?
c Why does Zwingli say that Luther has now been driven 'in an opposite direction' (line 15)? How far do you agree with Zwingli's opinion on this point?
★ d Who were 'the wretched slaves' (line 23) and why was Luther advocating such violent action against them?
★ e What was the essential disagreement between Luther and Zwingli about 'the body of Christ' present 'in the Supper' (lines 34–5)?

8 Charles V Decides on War, 1546

(a) Charles V to his son, Philip

The religious question is in such a position and the confusion of
Germany so great that there is little hope that the Protestants, of their
own accord, will abandon their errors and return to the communion of
the Church. This has been proved by the experience of the past and,
5   recognising now how greatly the evil has spread and daily continues to
increase, it is evident that unless a prompt remedy be found, great
difficulties and troubles may result, amongst others the dangers to which
the Low Countries would be exposed by their proximity and
connection with Germany. The matter, moreover, is signally for the
10   service of Our Lord, the increase of His Holy Catholic Faith, and the
quietude and repose of Christendom, to which we are so especially
bound by the dignity to which God has elevated us. And although we
have exerted ourselves to the utmost to remedy the evil, exposing our
person to so many troubles thereby, nothing has yet been effected
15   owing to the Protestants' obstinacy. . . . Besides this, the opportunity
which now presents itself should be taken advantage of. We have not
only settled the truce with the Turk, but the French have their hands full
with the English, besides being in great poverty; and our position
towards them is such that it is not probable they would attempt in
20   Germany what at another time they might. We are, moreover, well
armed and prepared for whatever may happen; this being a most
important point. On consideration of all these reasons and others, and in
view of His Holiness' offer of aid . . . which will produce a large sum,
we conclude that the amount promised by the Pope, with some other
25   funds which we hope to obtain, will be sufficient to cover the estimated
cost of maintaining the army for the necessary period.

> *Letters and Papers (Spanish)*, VIII, p. 306, in Martyn Rady,
> *The Emperor Charles V*, 1988, pp. 112

(b) Charles to His Sister, Mary of Hungary

My dear sister! . . . Since arriving here [Germany], I have worked
ceaselessly and through all possible means to bring the Lutherans and
others round to the way of peace and accommodation but, for all this,
30   nothing profitable has been achieved. As you've already heard, they
have recalled their deputies from the religious talks and not sent any
replacements . . . . And I have learnt that the electors, Landgrave and
others have decided between themselves not to attend the Diet. I am
informed from several quarters that they, anticipating matters will be in
35   confusion and complete disorder after the Diet, intend to do the
following: to work out a one-sided and partisan [religious] settlement
which they will then impose unilaterally on the rest of Germany, so
undermining imperial authority; to bend all to their will and wipe out
those who do not conform; to bring about the ruin of the Catholic
40   clerisy; to do all they can and yet more against the King, our brother,

and myself . . . . Having treated on these matters several times with our brother by letter, and in person since he arrived here, and also with the Duke of Bavaria, we are all agreed that there is no other means of resisting the Lutherans than force.

> Karl Lanz, *Correspondenz des Kaisers Karl V*, II, 1845, pp. 486–8, in Martyn Rady, *The Emperor Charles V*, 1988, pp. 112–13

Questions

a What was Charles' 'experience of the past' (line 4)?

b What other name was often given to 'the Low Countries' (line 8)?

c What justifications does Charles give Philip for his decision to go to war against the Protestants? Why do you think Charles was concerned to explain his decision so clearly and simply to his son?

d What other justification does Charles give his sister?

★ e What position was held by Mary of Hungary and how might she therefore be affected by Charles' decision?

★ f Who was 'the King, our brother' (line 40) and why was he entitled to be called a 'King'?

9 Some Decrees of the Council of Trent

On the Institution of the Priesthood. Sacrifice and priesthood are, by the ordinance of God, in such wise conjoined, as that both have existed in every law. . . . And the sacred Scriptures show, and the tradition of the Catholic Church has always taught, that this priesthood was instituted
5 by the same Lord our Saviour, and that to the apostles, and their successors in the priesthood, was the power delivered of consecrating, offering, and administering His Body and Blood, as also of forgiving and of retaining sins.

On Transubstantiation. And because that Christ, our Redeemer,
10 declared that which He offered under the species of bread to be truly His own body, therefore has it ever been a firm belief in the Church of God, and this holy Synod doth now declare it anew, that, by the consecration of the bread and of the wine, a conversion is made of the whole substance of the bread into the substance of the body of Christ our Lord,
15 and of the whole substance of the wine into the substance of His blood; which conversion is, by the holy Catholic Church, suitably and properly called Transubstantiation.

Decree concerning the Use of the Sacred Books. The same sacred and holy Synod, – considering that no small utility may accrue to the
20 Church of God, if it be made known which out of all the Latin editions, now in circulation, of the sacred books, is to be held as authentic, – ordains and declares, that the said old and vulgate edition, which, by the lengthened usage of so many ages, has been approved of in the Church, be, in public lecures, disputations, sermons and expositions, held as

25   authentic; and that no one is to dare, or presume to reject it under any
      pretext whatever. Furthermore, in order to restrain petulant spirits, it
      decrees, that no one, relying on his own skill, shall, – in matters of faith,
      and of morals pertaining to the edification of Christian doctrine, –
      wresting the sacred Scripture to his own senses, presume to interpret the
30   said sacred Scripture contrary to that sense which holy mother Church .
      . . hath held and doth hold.

      On Justification. If any one saith, that man may be justified before
      God by his own works, whether done through the teaching of human
      nature, or that of the law, without the grace of God through Jesus
35   Christ; let him be anathema. . . .

      On the Sacraments in General. If any one saith, that the sacraments of
      the New Law were not all instituted by Jesus Christ, our Lord; or, that
      they are more, or less, than seven, to wit, Baptism, Confirmation, the
      Eucharist, Penance, Extreme Unction, Order and Matrimony; or even
40   that any one of these seven is not truly and properly a sacrament; let him
      be anathema. . . .

      On the Eucharist. If any one saith, that Christ, given in the Eucharist
      is eaten spiritually only, and not also sacramentally and really; let him be
      anathema.

          L. Bernard and T. B. Hodges (eds), *Readings in European History*,
          1958, pp. 250–3

Questions

★   *a*   Explain how the decree on the Institution of the Priesthood
            (lines 1–8) differs from Luther's doctrine of the priesthood of all
            believers?

★   *b*   What was Luther's position on (i) transubstantiation (line 9) and (ii)
            the seven sacraments (lines 38–9)? How was his position repudiated
            by these decrees?

★   *c*   Why was the 'official' edition of the Bible called the 'vulgate'
            (line 22) and who else was put in a position of danger by this
            decree?

     d   What is meant by 'anathema' (line 35)?

★   *e*   Why would Luther have agreed with the decree on justification
            (lines 32–5)?

★   *f*   How does the decree on the Eucharist (lines 42–4) differ from
            Luther's position?

VIII   Attempts at Reconciliation

Luther's challenge to the teachings, and ultimately to the supremacy, of the pope could not be allowed to continue undisputed after 1517, especially when it became clear that his ideas were spreading so rapidly, largely thanks to the invention of printing. The pope and senior German churchmen were determined to make Luther recant or, if this should not be possible, to silence him. The Emperor Charles V felt that Luther deserved a personal hearing and so ordered his attendance at the Diet of Worms in 1521 and when this, too, proved unavailing and Luther had to be banned from the Empire, Charles still did not give up his attempts to reconcile him and his followers to the Catholic church.

There were, in fact, a considerable number of attempts at reconciliation in the years following Luther's publication of his ninety-five theses, even if some of them, such as the meeting with Cajetan, look more like attempts at coercion. Several of these attempts involved public meetings between Luther and his opponents, whether political like Charles V or ecclesiastical like Cajetan and Eck; others did not involve Luther personally, partly because he remained under the ban of the Empire and so was not free to attend public meetings in person and had to act through others, notably Philip Melanchthon, who was chiefly responsible for the Confession of Augsburg, presented to the Diet in 1530 (see also Chapter IV, extract 1) and also took part in the Diet of Regensburg in 1541, where the failure to achieve reconciliation led to Charles V's decision to resort to force.

A further problem was the development of other, rival, theologies, most importantly that of Ulrich Zwingli, who was seen by some as a rival to Luther. This rivalry meant that the challenge to the Roman Church was weakened, and therefore Philip of Hesse held the meeting at Marburg to bring the two reformers together, which, however, only ended by driving them further apart.

Finally the failure of all attempts at reconciliation was confirmed by the Treaty of Augsburg in 1555, which, for the first time, allowed two religions to co-exist within the Holy Roman Empire, even if only one was officially legal within each state of that Empire.

1   The Disputation at Augsburg, 1518

(a) Dear Spalatin, ... This is the third day since I arrived, nor have I yet seen the very reverend lord legate . . . . But although the very reverend cardinal legate himself promises to treat me with all clemency,

yet my friends will not allow me to rely on his word alone, so prudent
5   and careful are they. For they know that he is inwardly enraged at me,
no matter what he may outwardly pretend, and I myself clearly learned
this elsewhere. . . .

Yesterday he sent to me the ambassador of Montferrat, to sound me
on my position before the interview with himself. . . he pleaded with
10 me long, advancing arguments for sanity (as he called it), saying that I
should simply agree with the legate, return to the Church, recant what I
had said ill. . . . I said that if I could be shown that I had said anything
contrary to the doctrine of the Holy Roman Church, I would soon be
my own judge and recant. . . . Then he went on to make some insane
15 propositions, as, for example, he openly confessed that it was right to
preach lies, if they were profitable and filled the chest. He denied that
the power of the Pope should be treated in debate, but that it should be
so exalted that the Pope might by his sole authority abrogate
everything, including articles of faith, and especially that point we
20 were now disputing on. . . . Thus I hang between hope and fear, for this
clumsy go-between did not give me the least confidence.

> Martin Luther, October 1518, in E. G. Rupp and B. Drewery,
> *Luther: Documents of Modern History,* 1970, pp. 30–1

(b) To George Spalatin, Greeting. . . . This is now the fourth day that
my lord the legate negotiates with me, or rather against me. He fairly
promises, indeed, that he will do all mercifully and paternally, for the
25 sake of the most illustrious Elector, but in reality he wishes to carry all
before him with mere stubborn brute force. He would neither allow me
to answer him in a public debate nor would he dispute with me
privately. The one thing which he repeated over and over was: 'Recant.
Admit your error: the Pope wishes it so, and not otherwise; you must
30 willy, nilly'. . . .

At length he was with difficulty persuaded by the prayers of many to
allow me to present a written argument. . . . After some time he threw
aside my paper with contempt, and again clamored for recantation.
With a long and wordy argument . . . he thought to have conquered
35 and put me to silence. I tried to speak nine or ten times, but every time
he thundered at me, and continued the monologue. At length I, too,
began to shout. . . .

Thus the business stands. I have no hope nor confidence in him.

> Martin Luther, Augsburg, 14 October 1518, in P. Smith, *The Life
> and Letters of Martin Luther,* 1911, pp. 49–51

(c) To Cardinal Cajetan. Very Reverend Father in Christ, I come again,
40 not personally but in writing; deign to hear me mercifully. . . .

Now, Most Reverend Father in Christ, I confess, as I have before
confessed, that I was assuredly unwise and too bitter, and too irreverent
to the name of the Pope. And although I had the greatest provocation, I
know I should have acted with more moderation and humility . . . . For

45   so doing I am most sincerely sorry, and ask pardon, and will say so from
      the pulpit, as I have already done several times, and I shall take care in
      future to act differently and speak otherwise by God's mercy. Moreover
      I am quite ready to promise never to speak of indulgences again and to
      maintain silence, provided only the same rule, either of speaking or of
50   keeping silence, be imposed on those men who have led me into this
      tragic business.
         For the rest, most reverend and now beloved Father in Christ, as to
      the truth of my opinion, I would most readily recant, . . . if my
      conscience in any way allowed it. But I know that neither the command
55   nor the advice nor the influence of any one ought to make me do
      anything against conscience or can do so. . . .
         I humbly implore your Reverence to deign to refer this case to our
      Most Holy Lord Leo X, that these doubts may be settled by the Church,
      so that he may either compel a just withdrawal of my propositions or
60   else their just affirmation.
                     Martin Luther, 17 October 1518, in P. Smith, *The Life and Letters
                     of Martin Luther*, 1911, pp. 52–3

Questions

★   *a*   Why had Luther been summoned by Cardinal Cajetan, the
          'cardinal legate' (line 3) to Augsburg?
    b   What did the ambassador mean by 'filled the chest' (line 16)? What,
          in effect, was he arguing about the power of the papacy?
    c   Why does Luther say that Cajetan will act 'for the sake of the most
          illustrious Elector' (lines 24–5) and to whom is he referring?
    d   How do you account for Cajetan's tactics on this occasion?
    e   After the personal meeting between the two men, do you think the
          tone of Luther's letter to Cajetan would be persuasive?
★   *f*   How did public debates like this one actually help Luther's cause,
          whatever the outcome of the actual argument?

2 The Leipzig Disputation, 1519

Both sides arrived promptly. Eck came with only a single personal
servant, and with letters of introduction to our duke from the Fuggers.
Luther and Karlstadt brought with them the greater part of their
university. . . . Men of every estate gathered to see the debate, abbots,
5   counts and knights, learned and unlearned, so that this large university
had no hall big enough to accommodate such an audience. . . .
         Karlstadt and Eck, each asking the usual indulgence for himself,
descended into the arena. They debated on free will, that is what it has
to do with the work of salvation. . . .
10   Luther followed Karlstadt to sustain the thesis that it was only by
recent decretals that the Roman Church was proved to be superior to

other Churches, against which stood the authority of scripture and the Nicene Council. Eck left no stone unturned to overthrow this opinion; he summoned all the forces at his command, spending eight days on it and doing his best especially to make his opponent invidious by dragging in some Hussite articles. Luther at once understood the snare, and raged as though inspired by some spirit at being thus insidiously betrayed *on a side issue*. With great indigation he rejected some of the dogmas imputed to him, while embracing some of them as Christian, relying everywhere either on well weighed testimonies of scripture, or on the decrees of ancient councils. In short, his main effort was to remove far from himself the suspicion of favouring Bohemian schism. Eck also bent his whole energy on impressing the audience with this opinion of Luther, no matter how much the latter rejected it. In like manner they debated on other things, the state of souls in purgatory, fear as the root of penitence, and Indulgences, consuming nearly twenty days in all.

When they had finished each side claimed the victory. Eck triumphs in the opinion of all who like *asses playing the harp* do not understand the subject at all, . . . or who have some reason for wishing the Wittenbergers ill. The victory of Luther and Karlstadt is less acclaimed, because learned and judicious men are fewer and less confident in proclaiming their own opinions.

> Peter Mosellanus to Julius Pflug from Leipzig, 7 December 1519, in E. G. Rupp and B. Drewery, *Luther: Documents of Modern History*, 1970, pp. 34–5

Questions

a   Who was Eck (line l)? Who were the Fuggers (line 2)?

b   How did Luther attack the Roman Catholic Church when he 'followed Karlstadt' (line 10)?

★ c   What was meant by 'some Hussite articles' (line 16)? Why was this accusation such a 'snare' (line 16) for Luther?

d   Does the author seem to you to believe that Eck or Luther had achieved 'victory'?

★ e   Why was this disputation important for Luther and his ideas, apart from the immediate question of who 'won' the debate?

3   The Lutheran Revolt

(a) Brussels, 31 August 1520. To Pietro Martire d'Anghiera. That which you would fain learn from me, as to the origin and progress of the Lutheran sect, which has recently sprung up among the Germans, I am now about to write to you. . . .

For as a certain Dominican was preaching in Wittenberg, a city in Saxony, and urging the people to purchase these pontifical indulgences, from which this friar himself netted no mean profits, an Augustinian monk, of the name of Martin Luther, and the author of this tragedy, came forward, possibly moved by envy of the Dominican, and published certain printed propositions, in which he affirmed that the Dominican attributed to his indulgences effects much greater than the Roman pontiff either did or could concede. The Dominican, having read the propositions, was inflamed with wrath against the Augustinian, and the dispute between the monks was exasperated both by injurious expressions and by arguments – the one defending his sermon, and the other defending his propositions; so that the Augustinian, with the characteristic audacity of the wicked, began to disparage the papal indulgences, and to say that they had been devised, not for the welfare of the Christian body, but to satisfy sacerdotal avarice; and from this point the monk proceeded to discuss the powers of the Roman pontiff.

Then the Augustinian . . . declared that the temper of the Germans was getting irritated by long contemplation of the worse than profane habits of the Romanists, and that they had secretly begun to shake off the yoke of the Roman pontiff, which was accomplished when Luther's writings were first published, and received with general admiration and applause. Then the Germans, showing their contempt for the Romanists, evinced at the same time their intense desire, and they demanded it too, that there should be convened a general council of all Christians, in which, those things being condemned, against which Luther had written, better order might be established in the Church. . . .

(b) Worms, 13 May 152l. [Then Luther was summoned to the Diet of Worms, where the emperor], being unwilling to break his word publicly pledged for his safe-conduct, warned Luther by a published document that he should leave Worms on the day following, and that he should flee, within twenty days, to some place that might serve him as a refuge. Luther obeyed. The emperor, then, as well by his own authority as by that of the Prince Electors, and of all the Orders of the Roman Empire, having published an awful edict against Luther and the Lutherans, and against his writings, commanded that all the writings of Luther that could be found should be solemnly burned, and that, following his example, the same should be done throughout the other cities of Germany.

Here you have, as some imagine, the end of this tragedy, but I am persuaded that it is not the end, but the beginning of it. For I perceive that the minds of the Germans are greatly exasperated against the Romish See; and they do not seem to attach great importance to the emperor's edicts; for since their publication Luther's books are sold with impunity at every step and corner of the streets and marketplaces.

This evil might have been cured, with the greatest advantage to the Christian republic, had not the pontiff refused a general council, had he preferred the public weal to his own private interests. But whilst he obstinately stands upon his right, though possibly from a pious motive, or stopping his ears, he is anxious that Luther be condemned and burned at the stake. I see the whole Christian republic hurried to destruction, unless God Himself succour us. Farewell.

Alfonso de Valdes, in J. B. Ross and M. M. McLaughlin, The Portable Renaissance Reader, 1953, pp. 652–60

Questions

a   Explain what is meant by 'sacerdotal avarice' (line 19), 'the Roman pontiff' (line 20) and 'the Romanists' (line 23).

b   Who was the 'Dominican' (line 5)? Why is he so called and why is Luther referred to as 'an Augustinian' (line 7)?

c   In what ways had Valdes got the details wrong in extract (a)?

★   d   What was a 'safe-conduct' (line 33)? Why had one been issued to Luther by the emperor and why did some of Luther's friends warn him that a safe-conduct might not be sufficient protection when he set out for Worms?

e   Why did Valdes consider that the 'tragedy' (line 43) was only just beginning? How did he argue that it could be 'cured' (line 49) and why did it seem to him unlikely that this would happen?

4   The Marburg Colloquy, 1529

(a) Philip of Hesse to Zwingli, 22 April 1529

We are presently attempting to call together Luther and Melanchthon, as well as those who share your views concerning the sacrament. Perhaps the gracious and almighty God will bestow his grace so that on the basis of the sacred scriptures concord can be achieved concerning this article which would enable us to live in common Christian understanding. At this Diet the Papists attempt to support their false life and morals by insisting that we, who adhere to the pure and clear Word of God, are not of one accord concerning our faith. Thus I graciously request that you will eagerly do your part to bring together at an appointed time and place both you and the Lutherans so that, as I said before, the matter can rightly be brought to a Christian consensus.

(b) Luther to Katherine Luther at Wittenberg, 4 October 1529

Grace and peace in Christ. Dear Lord, Katie, know that our friendly conference at Marburg is now at an end and that we are in perfect union in all points except that our opponents insist that there is simply bread and wine in the Lord's Supper, and that Christ is only in it in a spiritual sense. Today the Landgrave did his best to make us united, hoping that even though we disagreed yet we should hold each other as brothers and members of Christ. He worked hard for it, but we would not call them

brothers or members of Christ, although we wish them well and desire
20 to remain at peace. I think tomorrow or day after we shall depart.

(c) Zwingli to Vadian, 20 October 1529

Grace and peace to you from the Lord.

I'll give you a brief account of what you are so anxious to learn.
When we had been brought to Marburg under most trusty escort, and
Luther had arrived with his own friends, the Landgrave decided that
25 there should be separate preliminary conferences in private, Oecolam-
padius with Luther and Melanchthon with Zwingli, to seek between
themselves for any possible measure of agreement that could lead to
peace . . . .

On the next day the four of us entered the arena in the presence of the
30 Landgrave and a few others – twenty-four at most; we fought it out in
this and in three further sessions, thus making four in all in which, with
witnesses, we fought our winning battle. Three times we threw at
Luther the fact that he had at other times given a different exposition
from the one he was now insisting on of those ridiculous ideas of his,
35 that Christ suffered in his divine nature, that the body of Christ is
everywhere, and that the flesh profits nothing; but the dear man had
nothing to say in reply – except that on the matter of the flesh profiting
nothing he said: 'You know, Zwingli, that all the ancient writers have
again and again changed their interpretations of passages of scripture as
40 time went on and their judgement matured.' . . .

The truth prevailed so manifestly that if ever a man was beaten in this
world, it was Luther – for all his impudence and obstinacy – and
everyone witnessed it, too, although of course the judge was discreet
and impartial. Even so, Luther kept on exclaiming that he hadn't been
45 beaten, etc. We have, however, achieved this much good, that our
agreement on the rest of the doctrines of the Christian religion will
preclude the Papal party from hoping any longer that Luther will come
over to them.

E. G. Rupp and B. Drewery, *Luther: Documents of Modern History*,
1970, pp. 135–9

Questions

a   Why did Philip of Hesse think that a meeting between Luther and
Zwingli and their friends was necessary? Why was Philip the person
to summon it?

b   What does Luther say was the only point on which agreement
could not be reached? How did his views of this topic differ from
those of Zwingli?

c   What evidence is there in the letters of both Luther and Zwingli to
explain the failure of the colloquy? Do you think Zwingli was
correct to say that Luther was 'beaten' (line 45)?

d What was Zwingli's opinion of Luther, as evidenced in extract **(c)**? What does he regard as the most important achievement of the occasion?

★ *e* What was the long-term result of the failure of Luther and Zwingli to agree?

5 The Original 'Protest'

Protestation read openly before the Electors, and submitted to the official records of the realm.

Your Worship, and you, dear lords, cousins, uncles, friends, and associates; you know what sort of grievance we caused to be presented,
5 both orally and in writing, on the final day of the recently held Diet, against certain points in the article about 'the preservation of peace and unity, in light of threatened divisions over religion in the realm, until a council is held to deal with it'. And although, in our presentation, we deliberately referred to nothing but what was demanded on the one
10 hand by our consciences, for the honour and praise of God and the hallowing of his name, and on the other by the inescapably urgent need of the said 'peace and unity' of the realm, Your Worship and you others ought to have searched for a way whereby with good conscience and without complaint we might have reached agreement with Your
15 Worship and you all in interpreting the last Recess of Speyer, if that Recess had indeed been 'abused' through differing interpretations. . . .

But since we have found that Your Worship and you all insist on maintaining your point of view; and since you reject our recital of the pressing causes and grievances which we want immediately restored and
20 repaired everywhere, both for conscience's sake, and because it appears that Your Worship and your excellencies will make no concessions, either officially or in any other way, for 'preserving peace and unity pending a council, in light of threatened divisions', nor take any action in which we can participate and assent; furthermore, both because of the
25 way the business was conducted, and, before that, because of the last Recess of Speyer cited above: we are not bound by this decision – especially since our consent was lacking. . . . We therefore conclude that, on the basis of our oft-repeated complaints, our extreme and inescapable necessity demands that we openly protest to your excellencies against
30 the declaration of Your Worship and of you all as void and without authority . . . and as not binding on us and ours, individually and collectively; and we do so protest by these presents. And we have hereby protested to Your Worship and to you all that for similar reasons we cannot, may not, and know not how to acquiesce in the said resolution
35 of Your Worship and of you others, but regard it as void and not binding. We wish nevertheless in the matter of religion, pending the said 'general and free Christian council or national assembly', with the help of the godly assistance, authorisation, and provisions of the much-

cited last Recess of Speyer, 'so to act, live, and rule' in our governments,
40 and also by and with our subjects and kinsmen, 'as we trust to give
account before God Almighty and His Roman Imperial Majesty', our
most gracious sovereign. In addition, the decisions concerning spiritual
taxes, rents, fees, and tithes, and those concerning peace drawn up and
published in the oft-mentioned last Recess of Speyer we wish to apply
45 and retain everywhere unaltered. Similarly, we wish it known that we
are of one mind with Your Worship and with you all on what the
following article asserts concerning re-baptism and its suppression, as we
have obviously been throughout this Diet; and that we hold the
provisions of this article to be entirely appropriate.

> Appeal and Protestation of some German Princes, Speyer, 1529, in
> L. D. K. Siggins (ed.), *Luther*, 1972, pp. 93–5

Questions

   a   The Emperor was not present on this occasion. Why was he absent
       and who, therefore, presided over the Diet and is referred to as
       'Your Worship' (line 3)?

★   *b*   What is the importance of the title 'Protest' and who were
       responsible for making the protest?

   c   'The Recess of Speyer' (line 15) (1526) had in effect allowed each
       German state to choose its own religion. How had it apparently
       been 'abused' (line 16)? Why do the authors of this document
       regard the decision taken at Speyer in 1529 as being 'not binding on
       us and ours' (line 31)? How do they want the German religious
       problem to be solved?

   d   What were 'tithes' (line 43)?

   e   What is the significance of the reference to 're-baptism and its
       suppression' (line 47)?

6   The Diet of Augsburg, 1530

(a) To that venerable man, lord Nicholas Nausmann, faithful and
sincere bishop of the church at Zwickau.

     Grace and peace in Christ! Our friend Februarius will report to you
better than I can write, good sir, everything that happened both at
5 Augsburg and here with me. Yet after he had arrived here to see me, Dr.
Jonas wrote that our Confession (which Philip prepared) was read
publicly in the imperial palace itself by Dr Christannus [Beier], our
Prince's Chancellor, before the Emperor and the princes and bishops of
the whole empire, with only a crowd of commoners excluded. And the
10 following subscribed the Confession: first, the Prince Elector of Saxony;
then Marquis Georg of Brandenburg; Prince Johann Frederick, Junior;
the Landgrave of Hesse; Ernst and Franz, Dukes of Lueneburg; Prince
Wolfgang of Anhalt; and the cities of Nurnberg and Reutlingen. Now

they are deliberating about the imperial response. Many bishops are
15 inclined to peace, and despise the sophists Faber and Eck. In private
conversation one bishop is reported to have said: 'This is the pure truth –
we cannot deny it.' Mainz especially is said to be anxious for peace.
Similarly, Duke Henry of Brunswick, who familiarly invited Philip to a
meal as a sign of friendship, testified that he certainly could not deny the
20 articles about two kinds in the sacrament, priestly marriage, and
unimportant distinctions of foods. Our people report that no one in the
whole Assembly is more accommodating than the Emperor himself.
New beginnings are signalled thus. The Emperor deals with our Prince
not only mildly, but also reverently; so Philip writes. It is marvellous
25 how everyone is burning with love and good will for the Emperor.
Perhaps, if God wills, just as the Emperor was the worst of men at first,
so here at last he will be the best of men! . . . The Lord be with you,
Amen. Greet all our friends. From the desert, July 6, 1530.
Your Martin Luther.

I. D. K. Siggins (ed.), *Luther*, 1972, pp. 95–6

(b) To Conrad Cordatus at Zwickau
30 Jonas writes me that he was present during the session when the
Confession was read before the Diet and supported in a two-hour
oration by Dr. Beier. . . . Our enemies certainly did their best to prevent
the Emperor allowing it to be read, and they did succeed in preventing
its being read in the public hall before all the people. But the Emperor
35 heard it before the princes and estates of the Empire. I am overjoyed to
be living at this hour, when Christ is openly confessed by so many in a
great public assembly and with so good a confession. . . . Do not cease to
pray for the good young Emperor, worthy of the love of God and of
men and for the not less excellent elector who bears the cross and for
40 Melanchthon who tortures himself with care.

Martin Luther, 6 July 1530, in P. Smith, *The Life and Letters of
Martin Luther*, 1911, p. 259

Questions

a Who were Philip (line 6), 'our prince' (lines 7–8) and Eck (line 15)?
b Who was referred to as Mainz (line 17) and why did his opinion
matter?
★ c Why was Luther not present in Augsburg himself? Do you think
his absence made any difference to the outcome of the meeting?
d What theological arguments are referred to as 'two kinds in the
sacrament' and 'priestly marriage' (line 20)?
e Why did 'our enemies' (line 32) want to prevent the Confession
from being read by the Emperor and why was it so important to
Luther that this should be done?

7   The Diet of Regensburg, 1541

(a) Parts of the reports by the Protestant envoy of Augsburg to his town council

4 May

From all the discussions to date, I have come to the conclusion that His Imperial Majesty is anxious, above all else, for a Christian settlement of religious matters and the maintenance of a just peace and security in the Holy Empire. We must freely thank Almighty God that in these hard
5   times His Godly Majesty has, despite all advice to the contrary, ordained our affairs in such a benevolent manner. God be still gracious to us!

There is in general nothing much to report except that the theologians are applying themselves eagerly in the religious negotiations and have reached agreement on the article concerning
10   justification . . . . Our side is delighted about this. God be eternally praised! Amen!

6 May

Yesterday, the theologians hit a crisis. The Catholics want to include transubstantiation in [the article concerning] Our Lord's Supper. Our theologians will not allow this. The subject will be broached anew in
15   today's discussions. It is to be feared that a split will develop on this issue because the reputation of the papacy hangs on it. Nor are our theologians prepared to back down, as transubstantiation goes against Holy Scripture.

7 June

In the religious discussions, the Emperor dearly wishes progress in those
20   articles which cannot be agreed upon. But our theologians have no wish to participate in more talks and therefore further agreement cannot be expected. . . . I warn you that His Imperial Majesty may perhaps impose his own arrangement.

9 July

The Protestant estates at the Diet have sent the *Book* to be read again by
25   all the preachers in attendance . . . . They are to decide what should stay in the *Book*, what needs to be contradicted or given further explanation, what goes against Holy Writ and the Confession of Augsburg; and they are to make the description of the Lord's Supper clear and expressive.

> *Archiv fur Reformationgeschichte,* III, 1905, pp. 18–64; ibid, IV, 1907, pp. 65–98, 221–304, in Martyn Rady, *The Emperor Charles V,* 1988, pp. 108–10

(b) To Philip Melanchthon at Regensburg

Grace and peace. Dear Philip, . . . I pray the Lord to guide and preserve
30   you from the wiles of Satan and especially from that [Philip of Hesse] and his ilk. Our good Elector yesterday sent me . . . that man's advice

about making peace with the Emperor and our opponents. I see they think this is a comedy of men instead of a tragedy of God and Satan. . . . I write with rage and indigation against those who trifle in such matters.
35 But thus it must be, for throughout history the Church has suffered, like St. Paul, the dangers of false brethren. . . . God knows who are his own. I would write more did I not know that you hate such men and measures as much as I. What do they mean by saying that we neglect the primary articles of faith to dispute about things indifferent? Is the Word
40 of God and the sacrament, in perverting which they tempt, slight, and insult God, a thing indifferent? Peace will be easy 'in things indifferent' if, by our impenitence, we relegate serious and important matters to this category.

> Martin Luther, from Wittenberg, April 1542, in P. Smith, *The Life and Letters of Martin Luther*, 1911, pp. 392–3

Questions

a   What is meant by 'transubstantiation' (line 17)? Why did the discussions seem likely to break down over this subject?

b   How does the author's attitude to the Emperor change during the course of the discussions and why?

★ c   What was the 'Confession of Augsburg' (line 27)? Who had been responsible for drawing it up and for what similar occasion?

★ d   How had Luther's attitude to Philip of Hesse changed since 1529 (see extract 4)? Who was 'our good Elector' (line 31) and why should Luther call him 'good'?

e   What was meant by 'things indifferent' (line 39)? How had this phrase offended Luther? What do you think Luther was expecting to be the outcome of the discussions?

8 The Peace of Augsburg, 1555

We, Ferdinand, by God's grace king of the Romans . . . . Whereas, at all the diets held during the last thirty years and more . . . there have often been negotiations and consultations to establish between the estates of the Holy Empire a general, continuous and enduring peace in regard to
5 the contending religions . . . to secure again peace and confidence, in the minds of the estates and subjects toward each other, and to save the German nation, our beloved fatherland, from final dissolution and ruin; we . . . have united and agreed with the electors, the princes and estates present. . . .
10 1. We therefore establish, will and command that from henceforth no one, whatsoever his rank or character, for any cause, or upon any pretence whatsoever, shall engage in feuds, or make war upon, rob, seize, invest, or besiege another. . . .
2. And in order that such peace, which is especially necessary in view of
15 the divided religions . . . and is demanded by the sad necessity of the

Holy Roman Empire of the German nation, may be the better established and made secure and enduring between his Roman Imperial Majesty and us, on the one hand, and the electors, princes, and estates of the Holy Empire of the German people on the other, therefore his
20 Imperial Majesty, and we, and the electors, princes, and estates of the Holy Empire will not make war upon any estate of the empire on account of the Augsburg Confession and the doctrine, religion, and faith of the same, nor injure nor do violence to those estates that hold it, nor force them, against their conscience, knowledge, and will, to abandon
25 the religion, faith, church usages, ordinances, and ceremonies of the Augsburg Confession, where these have been established, or may hereafter be established, in their principalities, lands, and dominions. Nor shall we . . . trouble or disparage them, but shall let them quietly and peacefully enjoy their religion, faith, church usages, ordinances, and
30 ceremonies, as well as their possessions, real and personal property, lands, people, dominions, governments, honors, and rights. . . .
3. On the other hand, the estates that have accepted the Augsburg Confession shall suffer his Imperial Majesty, us, and the electors, princes, and other estates of the Holy Empire, adhering to the old religion, to
35 abide in like manner by their religion, faith, church usages, ordinances, and ceremonies. They shall also leave undisturbed their possessions, real and personal property, lands, people, dominions, government, honors, and rights, rents, interest and tithes. . . .
5. But all others who are not adherents of either of the above-mentioned
40 religions are not included in this peace, but shall be altogether excluded.
6. . . By the authority of the revered Roman Imperial Majesty, fully delegated to us, we have established and do hereby make known, that where an archbishop, bishop, prelate, or other spiritual incumbent shall depart from our old religion, he shall immediately abandon, without
45 any opposition or delay, his archbishopric, bishopric, prelacy, and other benefices, with the fruits and incomes that he may have had from it. . . .
11. But when our subjects and those of the electors, princes, and estates, adhering to the old religion or to the Augsburg Confession, wish, for the sake of their religion, to go with wife and children to another place
50 in the lands, principalities, and cities of the electors, princes, and estates of the Holy Empire, and settle there, such going and coming, and the sale of property and goods, in return for reasonable compensation for serfdom and arrears of taxes . . . shall be everywhere unhindered, permitted, and granted.

J. H. Robinson, *Readings in Modern History*, Vol. II, 1906, pp. 113–16

Questions

a   Who was 'his Roman Imperial Majesty' (lines 17–18)? Why had he 'delegated' his 'authority' (lines 41–2) to Ferdinand and what was the significance of Ferdinand's title 'king of the Romans' (line 1)?